ABCs of Kindergarten

or

*Spice and Snails
and
Heir-Raising Tales*

by

Verna Chambers

Illustrated by
the author

Pearce-Sunsites Publishing Company, Inc.
Pearce, Arizona

ABCs of Kindergarten

or

**Spice and Snails
and
Heir-Raising Tales**

•

First Edition
1999
Copyright by
Verna Chambers

•

Cover Design and Drawings
by
the author

•

Printed and Bound in the
United States of America
by
Eerdmans Printing Company

•

ISBN 0-9665366-0-6
Library of Congress Catalogue
Number 98-066108

Acknowledgments

I hope this is an encouraging book for parents and teachers of young children, and that it will be an aid in understanding the developmental levels through which our children must progress. And I hope that parents, teachers, grandparents and everyone else will enjoy the unintentional humor that children often add to our lives as we laugh with them, but never at them.

I am indebted to Ellen Duhon, Judy Hemming, Esther Dixon, Margaret Estavillo, and Sylvia Turner who kept saying, "Verna, with all your years of experience you should write a book!" Thanks to the teachers whose classroom "funnies" I borrowed. My thanks go to Frank Jordon, Gene Lafferty, Bea Carlton and Loraine Shonting for their counsel and enthusiasm in my writing, and to Howard Shonting who convinced me that with my kindergarten-level style of drawing I could illustrate the book. I am grateful to those friends who spent hours proofreading for me, in particular Twila Shelton, Bennett and Marvel Noland, Joy Boyd, Margarette Lafferty, and especially my husband Clell. Thanks to Gary Horton, computer consultant, who typed and organized a large part of this book, along with his wife Eunice. Thanks also to Carmen Ronquillo, Chris Everist, and Ryan Macias, of Kinko's in Tucson, who converted the disks to one single Zip disk containing the entire book including the color illustrations. Also thanks to professional proofreader Elizabeth Ohm, who said, "It was a pleasure working on the manuscript." Thanks to Caryn Shonting for tieing all the ends together and ensuring the book made it to store shelves and the Internet.

And finally, Kathleen and Benny who didn't demand a bribe for allowing me to identify them by name as I related their childhood "funnies."

Willcox, Arizona

Willcox, Arizona, where the author taught school, is located in the southeastern portion of Arizona, in the northern half of Cochise County on Interstate 10, 80 miles from Tucson, 75 miles from Mexico and 40 miles from New Mexico at an elevation of 4,200 feet. Willcox is considered high desert; its economic base is agriculture.

Willcox was once known as the "cattle capital" of the nation, and cattle are still an economic important part of this area. Willcox has its own Cowboy Hall of Fame where its cattleman heritage is properly honored. The favorite nominee is Rex Allen, Arizona's "Mr. Cowboy," who was born and reared in Willcox and still considers Willcox his hometown. Willcox honors him by celebrating Rex Allen Days on the first weekend of October every year. Perhaps, though, the most noted residents of the area were the Apache warrior Geronimo and Chief Cochise.

In close proximity to Willcox are the Chiricahua National Monument, Old Fort Bowie, The Amerind Foundation Museum, Cochise Stronghold, the ghost towns of Dos Cabezas and Pearce, the Faraway Ranch, apple and pistachio orchards, emu farms, and the Willcox Playa Wildlife Refuge (where you can see sandhill cranes from October through February). These attractions provide a delightful and memorable experience for anyone who visits this southwestern enclave where the sun almost always shines. The Chiricahua Mountains are world-famous for bird watching.

Most of the people who live in Willcox feel there is no place in the world they would rather be. The ideal climate, the friendly relaxed lifestyle, and the economic and social atmosphere make it a unique place to live or visit. Perhaps a resident summed it up best when he said, "Willcox has just about everything you could want and what it doesn't have most people wouldn't miss anyway."

Dedicated

to the thousands of little
angels and imps
whose
antics and innocence
furnished
the anecdotes and incidents
for this book

What are little boys made of, made of?
What are little boys made of?
Snips and snails,
And puppy dogs' tails,
That's what little boys are made of.

What are little girls made of, made of?
What are little girls made of?
Sugar and spice,
And all that's nice,
That's what little girls are made of.

Introduction

This story is beginning at the end. After a long teaching career, I wrote a letter of resignation to the school superintendent and school board members that read as follows:
"Gentlemen:
I have been teaching my third generation of students for several years. However, I am not trying to set any kind of record, and I really think I should retire before I start hearing myself, in a voice quavering with age, saying to some child, 'Honey, did your great-grandmother tell you that I was her teacher?' Therefore, I hereby offer my resignation, effective at the close of this school year. Needless to say, I have enjoyed my years of teaching; otherwise, I would not have stayed so long."

So went my letter of resignation, written 41 years after I began teaching. I didn't intend to become a career teacher, and if anyone had told me in 1942 that teaching would be my life for 41 years I would have, figuratively speaking, beat my head against the wall. Not that I disliked my job; it just wasn't what I had in mind. I envisioned teaching for the duration of World War II, then marrying the soldier I was engaged to, and after that the vine-covered cottage bit. Only in my case, the Arizona ranch bit.

I graduated from Arizona State University at Tempe in 1942, with a degree in home economics and a science major. I taught at the high school level in those areas for four years and loved it. Although I was scarcely older than my students and looked younger than my 20 years, discipline was never a problem. That was before the "era of disrespect" began. I married at the beginning of my third year of teaching.

When my husband came home from the war I completed the school year and then quit teaching. But come September, the nearby Arizona State Industrial School (actually a "correctional school") needed a full-time substitute for a few months. I found myself teaching students ranging from 11 to 17 years of age but at the third-and fourth-grade level. The following year I was hired as a regular teacher for students of the same age range who functioned at the fifth-or sixth-grade level. At the close of that year I quit again.

The next year our first child, Kathleen, was born, and small children became immensely more interesting to me than older ones. When the following year found us back in Willcox, the school needed a half-time junior high sewing teacher and a half-time kindergarten teacher, and there I was! My home economics major had given me the required background in child development to qualify for kindergarten certification. After holding this position for two years I left for the birth of my son Benny. After being out two years I returned to teaching and stayed with it.

I remained for 29 more years, a total of 37 years of teaching. I taught during a time that brought many changes to our country, our lifestyles, and our schools. Any change in one is reflected in the others.

I have learned a great deal about children, parents, teachers, administrators, janitors, and humans in general. It is my purpose to share some of the smiles, tears, foibles, and a few of the things I learned about dealing successfully with children.

I am fully aware that children and teachers come in both sexes, and I haven't the slightest prejudice against either. But for the sake of clarity, when speaking in generalities, I have referred to the child as **he** and the teacher as **she**. If I deviate in a specific case it will be obvious from the context.

While most of the anecdotes included in this book happened in *my* classroom, I have borrowed a few from other teachers' experiences. The "recipes" are attributed to the students who supplied them. Otherwise, I have changed the names and some times the gender of all individuals mentioned throughout this book, as my daughter says, "to protect the guilty." My children, Kathleen and Benny, weren't granted this protection!

Acknowledgments		*iii*
Willcox, Arizona		*iv*
Dedication		*v*
Introduction		*vi*
Chapter 1	Believe It or Not	10
Chapter 2	The Mangling of the Language	15
Chapter 3	Ready for Kindergarten?	19
Chapter 4	First Day of School	25
Chapter 5	Please Excuse Johnny	30
Chapter 6	Rumpelstiltskin	33
Chapter 7	Gross Goodies	39
Chapter 8	Reading Readiness and Green Tomatoes	42
Chapter 9	There Are No Secrets	46
Chapter 10	The D Word: Dyslexia	49
Chapter 11	More Mangling of the Language	54
Chapter 12	Phonics Phun	57
Chapter 13	It's Only Logical	61
Chapter 14	Making Little Things Count	65
Chapter 15	Story Translations and Transmutations	69
Chapter 16	Do-Re-Mi-I-E-I-O	72
Chapter 17	Nature Lessons from Children	76
Chapter 18	The Field Trip That Wasn't	79
Chapter 19	Amateur's Analysis of Amtrak	82
Chapter 20	*A* is for Art	85
Chapter 21	The View from 45 Inches	91
Chapter 22	Aides and Anna's Bananas	95
Chapter 23	Git Along, Little Dogies	98
Chapter 24	What Did You Do Today?	104
Chapter 25	Zoo's Who?	107
Chapter 26	Ma, Your Manners Are in the Mirror	112
Chapter 27	The Parents Responsibility?	115
Chapter 28	My Mama's Name Is Mama	120
Chapter 29	Ghost Feathers and Cow Stuff	122

Chapter 30	The Big D — Discipline	126
Chapter 31	Mary, Mary, Quite Contrary	138
Chapter 32	Kindergarten Stew	141
Chapter 33	Little Round Green Things	144
Chapter 34	I Wasn't Eavesdropping	150
Chapter 35	Teacher's Pet	154
Chapter 36	He Grew Germs Off Us	160
Chapter 37	Thank You for This Feud	163
Chapter 38	Show and Tell	169
Chapter 39	Questions, Pertinent and Impertinent	173
Chapter 40	Kate and Dupli-kate	177
Chapter 41	Love Offerings	180
Chapter 42	So Who Is Handicapped?	183
Chapter 43	Oats, Peas, Beans, and Barley Grow	189
Chapter 44	Get Along with *Who*?	195
Chapter 45	We Had Fun at the Dentist's Office	198
Chapter 46	Some Things You're Never Prepared For	201
Chapter 47	Real People?	204

| Works Cited | 213 |
| Autobiography | 214 |

Chapter 1

Believe It or Not

My experiences and observations, based on nearly forty years in the classroom, are that small children are basically truthful as far as their perception, understanding, and vocabulary permit. Nevertheless, on the first day of school my students always went home with letters pinned on their backs which, in addition to information pertinent to my classroom mode of operations, gave this admonition to the parents:

"Please don't believe everything your child tells about school and I won't believe everything he tells about home!"

Of course, some children have learned to lie from watching others, or sometimes from deliberate coaching. And any child is apt to lie if he feels that it will extricate him from a threatening situation, such as being caught in a misdeed. Still, there is usually some basis of truth in what they say.

They may misconstrue what they have seen or heard. Sometimes they simply don't have the proper vocabulary to convey their meaning. Or perhaps the statement or story is out of context, giving it a different slant. And sometimes the child simply uses the wrong word, one that sounds similar to the intended meaning. Some tell tall tales because they have an overactive imagination, or perhaps as an attention-getting device. Also, until about four or four-and-a-half years of age children sometimes don't quite distinguish between reality and fantasy. The humorous accounts in this book are some of the more memorable ones I've heard from my students over the years.

* * *

Tommy, from a single-parent home, was bragging about Daddy's culinary skills and how much he liked it all. "I eat 'most everything Daddy cooks. I'm very easy to please. I eat beans and tacos and oatmeal. And I even eat lizards!" (Did we call Child Protective Services? No, because he meant gizzards.)

* * *

Upon Kristi's arrival at school she rushed into class and reported, "Teacher, my daddy killed my mama last night. He killed her and buried her under the porch!"

The teacher couldn't believe it and tried to talk the child out of her story, but she stuck by it. So the teacher discussed it with the principal. They decided to report it to the police and let them investigate the matter. Using some pretext to go to the child's home, the police knocked on the door and there was Mama without even so much as a scratch or a black eye.

We will never know what prompted that story. Was it the child's imagination, something from television, a bad dream that seemed too real, a bid for attention, or an out-and-out lie? I suspect it was for attention.

* * *

In one class that I taught, several children had little brothers or sisters at a very interesting stage where new accomplishments were achieved almost daily. So we frequently heard about the little siblings: "Teacher, you know what? My little brother took his first steps yesterday." Or "Mine is learning to talk. He says dada."

Betsy always had a story about her little brother, reported with authentic-sounding details. I listened with special interest to Betsy's reports, watching for some discrepancy, great unlikelihood, or contradiction. After this had gone on for some time, whenever she told me about her little brother, I would ask a few questions, such as his name and age, or for further details about the event. It all sounded very accurate, but I knew the family well; she didn't have a little brother! She was the baby of the family. Obviously, a kindergarten case of keeping up with the Joneses!

* * *

Donnie Mills was hurt and angry with his grandmother. In speaking of her he usually called her "Mam-maw" or "Mam-maw Agnes," but today he took the formal approach. "Mrs. Chambers, may I tell you something? You know that Mrs. Mills, she told a lie on me. She said I broke her lamp, and I didn't do it. Mrs. Mills told a lie on me! And I'm not going back to her house until she cleans up her act!"

* * *

Becky reported, "My mommy just loves oatmeal. She just eats oatmeal all day long. Not just for breakfast, but *all day long*! She just takes out her false teeth and eats oatmeal!"

* * *

The word *faint* came up in class, and the children seemed unsure of its meaning. Larry explained, "Faint means kinda like you're standing there and all of a sudden you kinda go to sleep and fall over."

Jerry said, "Oh, I know about that. That's what my mom does when she gets drunk!"

* * *

My Weekly Reader[1] showed the picture of a dog with her four new puppies. In discussion of the picture with the kids, it was mentioned that the dog was really smiling with pride and joy over the new puppies. The teacher said, "Yes, the dog looks very happy about her puppies. And that's the way most mommies feel about their babies. They're really proud and happy."

Little Ike spoke up, "Well, *mine* wasn't. Not with me, and not with my little brother."

"Well, Ike, what makes you say that?" she asked. (Since Ike and his brother had been abandoned by their mother and were being raised by their grandmother, the teacher thought she'd opened a real can of worms.)

"Well," said Ike, "when I used to nurse, I would bite her, and so did my brother. And she wasn't very happy about that!"

* * *

One morning Tanya approached me with a rather troubled face and said, "My mom was feeding my little brother this morning, and do you know what my daddy said to my mom as he left for work?" I was aware there were marital problems here and didn't care to pry, but the child seemed to need to talk, so I said, "No, what did he say?"

"He said, 'Don't make that little boy eat that garbage!'"

Garbage? Curiosity took over, so I asked just what it was that Mama wanted Little Brother to eat. Didn't seem too bad. It was just oatmeal. But this sounds like a sure way to start an eating problem.

* * *

And then there was Tommy who tried so hard *not* to tell what happened at home. "Mrs. Chambers, do you know what?... No, Mom said I musn't tell, so…I mean, something happened — er—guess what happened to our fence…No, I'm not supposed to tell. My Mama told me not to tell, and she would be mad. But—maybe I could tell *you* what happened to our fence. No, I'm not supposed to tell…but… "

I said, "Tommy, if your mom said not to tell, then you shouldn't."

Tommy said, "No, I musn't tell. Mama would be mad, so I won't tell. But I'll just say this: Something happened to our fence, and me and my brother, we ain't ne-e-ever gonna play with matches no more!"

* * *

After a field trip to the police station, the subjects of robbery, burglary, and theft came up. Two or three children gave little tidbits about thefts or burglaries which had affected them. Then another child gave this enlightening contribution: "When my mother cleans house for people she always steals some things."

* * *

As you can see, it would not have been reasonable for me to believe everything I heard. What I did believe completely was a child's body language. A child who cringed or dodged whenever I spoke his or her name told me something, as did a child who totally "fell apart" whenever he made a mistake. And I remember the child from a questionable home situation, for whose mother the kindest description would be unstable. On the days Mark sat and sucked the first two fingers of his left hand while twisting his ear with the right, I knew things were not good at home.

I know I promised not to believe *everything* a child told me, but I didn't promise not to believe *anything*. Sometimes body language tells more than words.

Chapter Two

[2]The Mangling of the Language

    This incident is from a colleague's experience when she was teaching in an isolated ranching area. One morning an obviously upset mother came in and demanded of the teacher, "I want to know, just how are you teaching arithmetic to my little boy?"
"What do you mean, how do I teach arithmetic?"
"Well, the way he recites his addition facts. How do you have the children say that?"
"Oh," said the teacher, "I teach them to say 2 plus 2, the sum of which is 4; 2 plus 3, the sum of which is 5, and so forth. Why?"
A look of relief passed over the mother's face as she said, "Oh, I think I understand. He insisted that it was 2 plus 2, the *sonovabitch* is 4!"
Was there ever a person who didn't occasionally get his words twisted? We all do, and children are especially adept at it. Among my most delightful kindergarten gems are the word twists and substitutions they sometimes invent.
For instance, did you ever *really* listen to children saying the pledge to our flag? In spite of the time and effort I put into explaining the meaning of each word and phrase, not to mention a session on pronouncing the new or difficult words, what

I would hear was some variation of this:

"I plague a legion to the flag of the new nightie states of a miracle, and to the public for witches stand, one nation under guard, invisible, with liver, tea, and just us four walls."

And as one small boy concluded, "And that's the way to pollute the flag!"

* * *

Betty, age six, and Bobby, age four, had been to the mortuary to view their deceased grandmother. When Bobby said, "They had her in a nice big box," his older, and ever-so-much wiser, sister corrected him, "No, not a box. They had her in a casserole!"

* * *

Tony: "Mrs. Chambers, do you know what? Jan's brother bit my dog. I mean, Jan's dog bit my brother."

Jan: "Yes, my dog bit his brother, so we had to take it to the dog jail. You know…the *hound*!"

* * *

It was the middle of the last week of school, and I had begun clearing the room for the summer. When little Art came in and saw the bulletin boards all bare, he exclaimed in surprise, "Hey, look! Our room is bald-headed!"

* * *

This incident must be prefaced with two bits of background information. First, one of the popular grocery stores in Willcox, the town where I taught, was called Rey's Market, and was usually referred to simply as Rey's. And second, Willcox's foremost and favorite Local Boy Made Good is Rex Allen, Sr. He has a wonderful singing voice, fantastic range, and he specializes in authentic western ballads.

Also, he starred in a number of western movies, as well as in the TV series "Frontier Doctor." Rex Allen's voice has been used in a number of Walt Disney's documentaries. His style is unique, and once you hear his narrating, you always recognize it. So folks proudly proclaim that "Rex Allen was *born and raised* in Willcox."

This led one child to ask, "Why was Rex Allen born in a grocery store?"

I said, "Oh, no! What makes you think Rex Allen was born in a grocery store?"

He replied, "Well, everyone says he was *born at Rey's* in Willcox!"

* * *

On the playground Cindy said, "Let's play Duck, Duck, Goose, and I'm the gooser."

* * *

At one time we were instructed to begin our classes each day with a one-minute quiet moment which was officially referred to as a *Moment of Meditation*. One morning I forgot and started to go right into the lesson. But I was reminded by little Johnny who asked, "Teacher, aren't we going to have our moment of *womanization*?"

* * *

As we were taking a walk the children noticed some rattle-weeds growing beside the path.

Sandy: "I like those weeds 'cause you can stomp on them and they make a loud pop. They just pop, pop, pop."

Freddie: "Yeah, I know. That's why they're called *poppies*."

* * *

The discussion was about playground equipment. Tina told us, "My favorite thing to play on is the *Hershey* bars."

* * *

Sarah: "The Pilgrims came to America on a ship called the Safflower."

Peter: "Huh-uh, it was called the Cauliflower."

* * *

Ken: "Hey, Teacher, guess what I had for lunch. Straw!"

Teacher: "Straw?"

Ken: "Yeah, straw. You know—Mom makes it from cabbage—cabbage *straw*!"

* * *

Julie's father liked to sing and always sang around the home. He sang hymns, classics, popular songs, ballads—whatever. A favorite was "I'm in the Mood for Love." And it was only natural for little Julie to imitate what she heard, or at least try to. But what we overheard Julie singing was "I'm in the *Nude* for Love!"

Chapter 3

Ready for Kindergarten?

For admittance to kindergarten, the only ticket required by many schools is a birth certificate and an immunization record with a warm body attached. However, more and more schools now require a "readiness" or "maturity" test for admission or placement in kindergarten. This is in contrast to the requirement when I first began teaching. If a child who was presented for school appeared to be a little underage, we checked his teeth! If he hadn't lost any baby teeth, he was deemed too young for school.

Now, no one wants Johnny or Joanie to "flunk sandbox" before they even start, so what can a parent do to help the child be ready for kindergarten? I'm not suggesting teaching a child calculus, or even reading. I'm speaking of helping a normal, average (if there is such), happy, well-adjusted preschooler become a happy, well-adjusted, progressing kindergartner.

Ideally, this preparation would begin on day one of the child's life. I realize none of us live in Ideal Land, but we can try to come as close as our circumstances permit. Ideally a child would have two loving parents, some siblings, a stable home in a safe environment, adequate food, clothing, medical care, appropriate discipline when needed, and ample opportunities for physical, mental, emotional, and spiritual development.

Assuming those needs have been met to the best of the parent's ability, what specific things should be addressed? I strongly suggest the following:

1. ***Development of muscle coordination***. Running, jumping, climbing, tricycle riding, or dancing for the large muscles. For small muscle coordination use crayons, scissors (blunt-nosed), Tinkertoys, Legos, puzzles, etc. (Battery-operated toys don't do much for development of coordination.) Remember, strange as it may seem, proper muscle coordination seems to play an important part in a child's ability to learn to read.

2. ***Observation skills***. Most children need help in interpreting mentally what their eyes see. Thus, parents need to call a child's attention to items in his surroundings and explain what purpose they serve. For example, a mother who was taking her daughter's Brownie troop to Tucson happened to comment, "There's quite a breeze blowing; look at how that windmill is whirling."

Some of the girls who had lived all their lives in this area where windmills are common didn't know that those things were called windmills, or that their purpose was to pump water for the cattle, or for houses if the ranch was so remote it didn't have electricity. Their parents never talked to them about the things they saw. So whether it's city sights, rural vistas, or just around the home, children need a little coaching on observation skills.

3. ***Listening skills***. Can he be attentive to short stories or nursery rhymes? Read to your child. He will enjoy it and learn from listening. Besides, it's a wonderful way to help your child relax at bedtime. And what better way to show your child that you love him and he is important to you? Tapes and records of children's songs and stories are good, but they lack the personal touch.

Another listening skill: can he follow a two-part set of directions, as in, "Shut the door, then bring me that book"?

4. ***Clear speech.*** Most five-year-olds' talk sounds a little *mushy*. Can non-family members understand them? Kindergarten teachers are experienced in understanding five-year-old-talk; if *she* can't understand Johnny or Joanie, there is a problem. More about speech a little later.
   5. ***Counting.*** They should be able to count at least to five, and to count objects with one number per object.
   6. ***Color recognition.*** They should be familiar with the basic colors. Never mind about magenta or chartreuse.
   7. ***Bathroom skills.*** Can he manage his own clothing, blow his nose, and wash his hands?
   8. ***Social skills.*** Taking turns, sharing, basic courtesy. Opportunities to be with other children their age, such as play school and Sunday school, are wonderful. Most children under four years can play socially side by side, but don't play *together*. By five years they should be able to interact in play.
   9. ***Personal information.*** Before beginning kindergarten each child should be able to tell his correct name, address, and parents' names, and to dial his home phone. Yes, even if your number is unlisted.
   10. ***A positive attitude about school.*** Which means that parents should display a positive attitude about school, even if they may have had some unpleasant experiences in school. Haven't we all? But one bad experience doesn't make the whole thing bad. And never, *never* say, "That teacher will whip you." It just ain't so!

   These suggestions should help your child arrive at school in a good frame of mind, ready for a great kindergarten year. Did someone ask, "If I have taught my child all that, what is the teacher going to teach him?" The answer is, "Plenty!"
* * *
   About Speech. Don't worry if your five-year-old still has a lisp (substitutes a *th*-sound for the s-sound, as in "I *with* I had a *thanwich* for *thupper*"). Or if he can't make an l-sound

or r-sound. (The usual substitution for these is a w-sound, as in "I *wuv* you," and "*Pwease wead* me a *stowy*." Many children don't master these sounds before six-and-a-half or seven years of age.

If Johnny has one of these problems, and his hearing is normal, and a parent wants to work with him, here are two suggestions:

(1) Work on only one sound at a time. Ignore all other mispronunciations he may have until this one is completely corrected.

(2) Sit down with the child in front of a mirror which is large enough for him to see both persons' faces. Show him how you shape your lips and tongue when making that sound. If he gets his lips and tongue shaped and placed right, the sound has to come out right.

Have a list of words that begin with that sound for him to repeat after you, making sure the lips and tongue are right. Correct him when needed, but don't make a federal case of it. And, above all, don't nag! You may wish to use a tape recorder so he can hear himself, but he probably won't believe that it's his voice, even if he just finished speaking into the recorder. (A camcorder would be more convincing.) If his speech is so immature that non-family persons cannot understand him, Johnny may be a good candidate for speech therapy.

I recall a first day of school when, upon sorting out enrollment forms and children, I found I had *one* small boy and *two* enrollment forms unmatched. I was sure the boy should match one of the forms, and asked him his name several times, but couldn't understand his reply.

Then I tried another tactic. Referring to the two forms, I asked, "Is your name George Johnson?" He garbled something. "Is your name Wilbur Smith?" Another garble. Since no other teacher came looking for a misplaced child, I was sure he must belong in my class. But who was the mystery child? During the day I alternately called him George, and then Wilbur, thinking I would be able to determine which name he responded to. I finally decided he must be George, and that was the name I wrote on his coloring paper. But when a mother claimed him at dismissal time she brought back his paper saying, "Wilbur got someone else's paper. This one says George."

Then I knew—he was Wilbur! But it took weeks, yea, months for his speech to improve enough for me, or anyone else, to guess what he might be saying. This was before the days of resident speech therapists. By the end of the year his speech passed for English, though barely.

There were three younger children in that family, and they all began school with extremely immature speech, though none was as bad as Wilbur's. All had normal hearing. Did their parents talk baby talk to them at home or encourage baby talk? Was the father such an ogre that they devised this method of speech so they could communicate without his understanding them? *Why* would a whole family of children reach school age and not be able to speak intelligibly? I don't know. But it behooves parents to speak distinctly to their children if they expect them to have proper speech development.

Little Betty was an immature child from what I would call a culturally deprived background, that of migratory labor. It was the first activity involving the use of scissors after she entered school in mid-fall. The other children immediately busied themselves with the project, but Betty just picked up the scissors with the utmost care and held them. I showed her what to do and got her started, or so I thought. Then I circulated around the room, giving help where needed, and was back to Betty in a few minutes. She had done nothing except sit and hold her scissors.

Once more I thought I had her started, but again, when I came back, there she sat, holding the scissors. I asked her, "Betty, why aren't you doing the cutting?" as, probably for the first time that morning, I really looked into her face. There I saw an expression of awe and pure ecstacy as she replied in a barely audible whisper, "This is the very first time I ever had scissors in my hand!"

So, don't make your children wait until kindergarten to have this thrill. Let them first experience it at home.

* * *

Age is not the telling factor as far as maturity goes. It is just a handy label. Most children do certain things at about the same age. For instance, most children begin walking at about 12 months, but some walk at nine months and some not until 18 months. It depends on their individual rate of maturity. Both are normal. But trying to *make* the 18-month walker walk at 12 months is useless and frustrating! Or trying to keep a 10- month-old walker off his feet will work only if you tie him down!

So it is with school readiness. If little Johnny shows signs of maturing more slowly than some children, encourage him, but don't push. The best thing Arizona ever did for kindergartners was to change the entrance age requirement from five years by December 31 to five by August 31. Among other things, that eliminated a lot of immature speech problems, most of the tears, and all of the wet pants!

For a child with an August birthday, unless he is obviously *very* mature, it may be in his best interest to wait another year. (*Sorry, parents and grandparents, you are too biased to be the best judges of their maturity.*) Likewise, if he doesn't score too well on his readiness admission test, regardless of birthday, allow him an extra year in which to mature. Call it a gift of time. The law doesn't say that he *must* enter kindergarten at age five, or first grade at six. It just says he can't enter before that age. It is better for the child to be the oldest one in his class instead of the youngest. And this is doubly true for boys. *Maturity* is the magic word!

Chapter 4

First Day of School

Who rates a 10? The mom who, on the first day of school, brings her child in, says, "Here's Willie Jones who has been assigned to your class. Willie will be just fine, I know. Now, Willie, I'll pick you up at yon gate at dismissal time. I'll see you then. Bye now." And then leaves *fast*!

At the other end of the scale is the mother who subconsciously wants her child to cling to her and cry, creating a trauma for the child in order to feed Mom's ego. It's called "See what a good mother I am. My child can't bear to leave me." Actually, once Mom is out the door and out of earshot, 99% of the time tears and noise disappear immediately, and the child is happy. Sometimes the child even gives the teacher a look that says, "Sorry about that, but I had to put on that act to please her."

Actually, the child's preparation for the first day of school should begin a few years earlier by leaving him with a babysitter occasionally, or by having him stay in the nursery at church. As a toddler he should spend time in his own Sunday school class or other type of group. Also, parents and older siblings should always speak of school in a positive light. I've heard parents say, "Well, I never liked school, so I don't think Susie will either." As if liking or disliking school was a hereditary trait, something in the genes. It's not, but a school attitude, good or bad, is certainly contagious. I remember a mother who said, "I just know Jane isn't going to like school. Children can be so cruel, and I know she'll be getting her feelings hurt." So, of course, Jane came home with a tale of woe every day. After all, Mother expected her to, and of course she got lots of attention and sympathy from Mother that way.

Much of the child's anxiety about beginning school can be allayed by taking him to see the classroom and playground in advance. In some schools this can be done on preregistration day in the spring, or perhaps before the opening day in the fall. It helps, too, if Johnny can meet the teacher ahead of time. Teachers are usually in their rooms about a week before classes begin.

* * *

Here is one of my favorite beginning-of-school stories. Little Cory sat and cried through day 1 of kindergarten even though I gave him plenty of lap time and told him how I knew his mom when she was small, and how I had taught his Uncle Danny. (That usually dispels any misgivings a child has, even makes him feel that he's special.)

Day 2 went much the same. Came day 3 and I again gave him a few minutes of lap time and tried to reassure him. My theory is if lap time and loving attention don't dry the tears, the child can cry in a chair by himself just as effectively. I sat Cory on a chair near my desk and turned to some paper work that required immediate attention. Then, suddenly and very unexpectedly, little Morris quietly approached Cory and said, "Cory, you shouldn't be crying. Kindergarten is going to be lots of fun. Why I've spent years and years just waiting to start kindergarten!"

* * *

Amanda was a little Navajo girl, and life off the reservation held many new experiences for her, things completely foreign. When an announcement from the office came over the intercom on the first day of school, she turned pale and her eyes grew big with wonder. I heard her whisper hoarsely, "The wall—it talks!"

* * *

Starting school is a traumatic experience for many children, and little Frank was no exception. He spent most of day 1 in tears, also day 2 and day 3. Came day 4, however, he was smiles all morning. When it was time to go home his teacher said, "Frank, did you forget something today?"

Frank replied, "Well, I forgot my jacket yesterday, but I remembered it today."

"What I mean is, did you forget to *do* something today?"

Frank looked puzzled but could think of nothing he had forgotten, so the teacher asked, "Didn't you forget to cry?"

With a big smile Frank replied, "Oh, I don't need to cry anymore. See here," and, fishing in his pocket, he pulled out a photograph. "My mom gave me a picture of herself, and told me that whenever I feel lonesome for her I could just take out the picture and look at it. That's what I did, and now I don't need to cry anymore."

What a clever Mom! She had helped Frank solve a big problem gently and without additional trauma.

* * *

Perhaps I seemed unfeeling in what I said about crying on the first day of school. Really, I understand why a child might cry briefly, especially if he has not had a chance to visit the classroom ahead of time, as perhaps on preregistration day. Usually these tears are quickly dried as he becomes interested in the classroom and activities. But if a child continues to cry day after day in kindergarten it would signify that either the child is not mature enough for school, even if the calendar says he is, or else it would indicate a very insecure child, or an emotional problem. And sometimes it is merely his way of manipulating people, of getting attention.

I remember Angela, bright, pretty, the oldest in her family. Mother walked her to school every morning, leading a four-year-old and a toddler and pushing a stroller with a 15-month-old, and looking like she had swallowed the Great Pumpkin.

Then, she walked back at noon to escort Angela home.

This had gone on for weeks. I kept wondering when Angela was going to assert her independence and come alone, or how Mama was going to manage when the new baby arrived. I talked with the mother about Angela needing to learn to walk to and from school by herself or with neighbor children. There were even others in our class who lived in the same block. But this approach got no results.

Now, Angela never cried when Mama left her at school; everything was fine until about 20 minutes before dismissal time, then the tears would begin. I supposed she had a fear of Mama not coming for her. No amount of reassuring seemed to help. She cried right on schedule every day. This went on for weeks and weeks.

A few times when Mama was a little late I pressured Angela to walk home by herself since she knew the way. But this made the matter worse. Once or twice she crawled right into the car with some other child and asked to be taken home. Of course, nothing bad happened, but I couldn't allow a child to think it was all right to get in the car with a stranger. She could have gotten into a serious, even fatal, situation.

One day in December, during music time, she turned on the waterworks right on schedule. Enough! I stood her up by the piano and said, "Now, cry! Cry all you want to; then keep crying." And I went ahead with the class's singing. If Angela quit crying I would command, "Cry!" without missing a note on the piano. She cried while the class sang. Ten minutes of this, and she got it all cried out. When dismissal time came, she paused only a moment at the gate and started walking home. Mama never had to escort her to or from school again. And she never cried again.

Then there was a first-grade class with a "bevy of bawling brats." First, there was Lydia, an "encore child" at home; not on the scheduled program since her siblings were all grown. She had been strictly a surprise. She was pretty, and badly spoiled.

Then there were the twins we'll call Pete and Repeat, and little Elnora, a Hispanic girl with limited English vocabulary. I had all four of these children in kindergarten the previous year; they knew I didn't bite. And in first grade I was careful to try to encourage and challenge children without putting undue pressure on them. But they cried more than they had in kindergarten.

Perhaps we would start the day fine. Then, for no reason at all, one of the quartet would decide to cry. That was the signal for the other three to join in. This went on for months, to the point of being ridiculous.

Finally, one day when it started again, I looked at the four of them: large, blonde Lydia, Pete and Repeat, and petite, brunette Elnora, all sitting there cross-legged on the floor in a circle, just bawling up a storm. This was enough! I just plopped down in their little circle, cross-legged like they were, and started my very loudest "boo-hoo-hooing." Instant silence from the quartet as they stared at me in wonder! I gave a few more "boo-hoo-hoos" for good measure, then looked up and said, "Didn't I look silly?"

They quietly got up and went to their places. No more tears for the rest of the year! (I should have done that sooner!)

Ecclesiastes 3:4[2] says there is "a time for tears," which, by inference, says there is a time when weeping is no longer appropriate, even for a five-year-old.

* * *

In summary, a happy first day of school most often hinges on preparing the child ahead of time mentally, emotionally, and socially; thus helping him to expect a pleasant experience and assuring him that his world of family and home is still there for him when school is over.

Chapter 5

Please Excuse Johnny

Notes that parents write are generally brief and to the point, expressing whatever is to be said in an unremarkable way. However, I have received a few that were different enough that I saved them. And sometimes the oral excuses given by children were memorable.

* * *

"Dear techer pleze excuze Johnny becaus of the circumstance beyon his control and due to the affect of the school if any questions ask me not him"

* * *

Ordinarily Lonnie's mom picked him up at school, but on the day he was to go to his grandmother's out on the farm I received this note: "Mrs. Chambers, Please put Lonnie on the bust. Thank you."

* * *

"Miz Chambers Kathy cain't bring no snack money cause I'm a-havin to git ready for my dautters wedding, and dont ast her no questions."

* * *

Among some of the verbal excuses I have heard are: "I couldn't come to school yesterday because we had to go to Bisbee to get my daddy out of jail."

"I didn't bring my snack money yesterday 'cause my mom got bit on the hand by a horse, and she couldn't write."

"I didn't come to school because I was in the hospital with ammonia."

* * *

"Mrs. Chambers, do you know why I was late? I missed the bus, and my daddy couldn't bring me to school 'cause he was already gone to work. And my mama couldn't bring me 'cause Daddy had the car. So do you know who brought me to school? My *father-in-law*" (his grandfather).

* * *

I thought little Hank's parents were a bit odd, and this incident confirmed my idea. Hank was a sickly-looking child, and when he returned to school after a two week absence without a note from Mom, I expected to hear him say that he had been ill. Not so.

"My daddy went to Pennsylvania. We had to take him to the airport."

"Oh, you weren't sick?"

"No, we took Daddy to the airport."

"But that would only take a day. You were gone two weeks."

Hank continued, "Yep, we took Daddy to the airport."

"Well, where were you the rest of the time?"

"At the airport. We had to wait there till Daddy got back."

"At the airport? What did you do? You had to eat and sleep."

"Oh, we slept in the car, and we ate crackers and cheese." It is less than a two-hour drive to the Tucson airport. They could have driven to Pennsylvania and back in less than two weeks.

I quizzed the child further, and was convinced that what he said was correct. Later discussion with the school nurse seemed to confirm it.

Today we hear of many homeless people, so this may not sound so shocking. But they weren't homeless. Here was a mother with three or four small children living in a car by choice for two weeks. The price of gasoline at that time was 35 cents a gallon. She could have driven home and fed the children better meals for less money, not to mention sleeping in beds. After that episode, I better understood what made Hank the odd little fellow that he was.

And a fellow teacher received this note:

"Please excuse Jerry's absence of yesterday. I gave him permission to miss school in order to participate in another activity which will help broaden his educational outlook. It consisted of placing a permanent identification mark on the posterior of immature bovine creatures by means of thermal instrument of appropriate temperature.

"Also, by the use of a keen instrument, the removal of a specific size and shaped portion of the animals' external auditory organs, and the removal of ossified epidermal growth from the animals' cranium. And from the male animals, the removal of certain portions of the anatomy not mentioned in polite society.

"This activity is sure to help Jerry learn how his parents make a living, indirectly from grass and other edible herbs according to the preference of said bovine animals. It will also help him learn to appreciate more fully the T-bone steaks and hamburgers which his dad provides and his mom cooks for him."

(The kid had been kept home to help brand, dehorn, castrate and earmark the calves.)

Chapter 6

Rumpelstiltskin

When parents name their children do they stop and think that the name is going to affect the child just as much as the face he wears? This is absolutely true. Perhaps you have read studies that report that the Erics and Erins get called on in class more than the Elmers and Effies and hence get better grades. Personally, I take a dim view of that accusation, but I do know that an unpopular or unusual name affects the way a child is treated by his peers. In some instances it can bring downright derision and scorn.

Back when I was in junior high, the subject of names came up, and all of us in the class told our middle names. There were three boys who went by initials: W.T. (William Thomas), J.B. (John Boyd), and P.K., who refused to reveal his real name. We begged and cajoled and guessed. If he had been really smart he would have said "yes" to Paul Kenneth or Peter Kevin, but he didn't. He finally said he would tell if we promised not to laugh. We solemnly promised, and promptly exploded with laughter when he told us: Plenty Kingdom.

I can't imagine the motivation for hanging that name on a child, but I can tell you the result. He was never again called P.K., but rather by his full name, at least by the boys in the class. They didn't dislike P.K.; it was just the "weird" name they found so amusing. Maybe those initials should have stood for Poor

33

Kid! As the result of all this he changed schools at the end of the semester.

Now, the other side of the story. When we named our daughter, we wanted a name that was common enough, but not too common, easily recognized, and with no spelling problems. We both liked the name Kathleen, and it seemed to meet the criteria. Well, we soon learned all the ways it could be spelled or misspelled. But little did we dream that *Kathy* was to become the Name for the Decade! Thus, our daughter has spent much of her life struggling to be called *Kathleen*. But, alas, she finally gave up and started going by Kate.

* * *

Duplicate names in a classroom usually don't cause a lot of trouble, but life is simpler without them, especially in kindergarten, and certainly before children learn to write their names. I remember dealing with three Garys one year, three Davids another. I especially remember a boy named Jon. His parents were quite smug about spelling his name, sans *h*. They had a rather long last name, so they economized on his given name. All was fine for awhile. He dutifully wrote *Jon* on all his paperwork. (This was first grade.)

Suddenly, he started forgetting to put his name on his papers. It soon became obvious that he wasn't forgetting, it was passive resistance. He just simply would not write his name unless I stood right over him. With 35 other first graders this was impossible. Finally, his mother, who was also a teacher, would stop by my room every afternoon to see if Jon had put his name on his papers. This involved checking through three or four stacks of worksheets, stacks of 35 each. If another child had forgotten his name, she would have to compare handwritings to guess which was Jon's. If there was no name, Jon watched no TV that evening.

This went on for several months, when, as suddenly as it had begun, the no-name game was over. His name was plainly there on every paper. And then the light dawned. It all began in November when a new boy entered our class, also named Jon. Both boys' last names began with *M*, so I asked them to add their middle initials when labeling their papers. Thus, it should be *Jon T.* and *Jon E.* Instead, I got *Jon T.* and a paper without a name. In April, Jon T. moved away, and Jon E. again named his papers—*Jon*, and after that there were no more orphan papers. When I analyzed the situation, it was clear that he had been made to feel that *Jon* was uniquely and exclusively his; no one else had a right to that spelling. Jon grew up to be a teacher and I wonder how many Jons he has had to share his spelling with. It has become a popular spelling and I've taught several more Jons over the years.

* * *

I always thought it best to call a child by the name he was comfortable with, usually by the name he was called at home. The exception was if the child was called by some nickname that had no relationship to his real name, or one that had unpleasant connotations, such as "Poochie" or "Stinky."

* * *

William was a very dignified child, very grown-up in his speech and usually able to express his thoughts precisely. This precision somewhat set me back on the first day of school when I asked dignified little William, "What would you like me to call you?" He looked somewhat confused, so I reworded my question, "What name does your mother call you? Does she call you William, or Billy? Or is it Will, or Willie?"

He answered very solemnly, "Well, I can give you an example. For instance, if it was time to eat she might say, 'Come to dinner, William.'"

And so from that day on he was William.

* * *

Then there was John Brown, which is all right here where he is known, but imagine when he's grown and moved elsewhere. "John Brown? Oh, yeah?" (Might as well be John Doe.) Also, there is the matter of expected teasing when the children sing "John Brown Had a Little Indian," as they certainly do when learning to count. I suggested to his parents that it would probably save him problems in the future if we used his middle name, Anthony. Thus, in kindergarten he was Tony Brown. But it didn't last; from first grade to this day, it is John Brown. And would you believe that when John Brown's sister married, John's new brother-in-law was named John Smith?

* * *

On a field trip to the police station, the policeman, after giving his talk to the children, opened the floor for questions or discussion. Eric raised his hand, and the officer, indicating Eric, asked, "Yes, sir?" Eric asked his question, listened attentively to the answer, and then said, "But next time, please call me Eric."

"Why?" asked the policeman.

"Because," said Eric, "that's my name."

* * *

One year there were five Kathys in my class. The first one to appear was Kathy. The second was called Kathy at home, but her name was actually Kathleen, so that's what we called her, rather than have another Kathy. Then, one by one, others appeared, and we had to add middle names. Thus, we had Kathy Ann, Kathy Lynn and Kathy Sue. The Kathys adapted to it nicely, but not so Kathy Sue's mom. She insisted that *her* child be the one called Kathy; let the first child add *her* middle name, which was — I don't remember — Clementine or Esperanza or such. Anyway, I couldn't see letting an unreasonable mother run my classroom. So although Kathy Sue's mother was very insistent when she said, "I don't *want* my daughter called *Kathy Sue*," the matter was finally settled when I asked her, "Then why did you name her that?"

* * *

If there is a moral to all this it must be: Remember, whatever you name your child, that's what he most likely will have to answer to all his life.

So, names should be chosen with a thought as to how they will be viewed by the child's peers. You may stand to inherit a fortune from Great Aunt Hephzibah if you name your daughter for her, but for the child's sake, make that the middle name.

In naming a child, the whole name should be said aloud several times to be sure it goes together well. For example, I'm not sure; is Lon short for Lorenzo? At any rate, I remember a neighbor, a Mr. Moore, whose peers all called him Lon, which in a western idiom would come out *lawnmower*.

I've heard my husband speak of a childhood playmate whose name was Ima Gray Foxx. My brother's classmate was a Native American boy whose last name was Rainwater, and he used initials for his given name: I.P. It is also true that I even went to school with Jack Frost!

One should also consider nicknames as well as initials and what they might spell. Consider the child whose unhappy mother, in order to spite the father (or unwanted child), gave her baby a name for which the initials were R.A.T.

* * *

One recent trend that I rather like is the increased popularity of biblical names for boys, and I've had them all from A to Z, literally. One year I had Adam and Zachariah. At another time when I called the roll it sounded like reciting the books of the New Testament—Matthew, Mark, Luke, John, Timothy, James and Peter.

We know that names come and go like dress styles. My personal feeling is to choose a middle-of-the-road name, not too new, not too old-fashioned; one that has a familiar ring, but is not too common. It is better to choose neither a name that must be spelled for people nor the "in" name of the year. I speak from experience here; Verna is a simple name, but I've spent most of my life spelling it for people. My late husband's name was Clell which is very simple, but he got called Clem, Cleo, Clay, Carl, and who knows what else. As far as spelling it goes, people couldn't seem to believe it contained three *l*'s! It appeared either as Clel or Cell so often that I had begun admonishing people, "Please don't knock the *l* out of Clell!"

Chapter 7

Gross Goodies

"Does she know how to cook?" was the reaction of my kindergartners when they learned that one of the sweet-young-things on our faculty was getting married. Some of the children were sure that they could give her some tips on cooking, and they were even willing to share some of their secret recipes with her. And since they shared with her, I'll share with you.

These recipes were recorded exactly as given by the children, and while some may be a little short on ingredients, they make up for it in imagination. Some of their recipes include ingredients that are quite difficult to find in local supermarkets. Perhaps these special ingredients are what makes the recipes "secret." Where do you find busketti? Or soaking powder? And "maglasses"—sounds like something from the optometrist.

Cooking temperatures vary, with most children opting for safety—very safe, even for ice cream, like four degrees. And the cooking times recommended are amazing.

It is definitely recommended that these be taste-tested before serving to guests. And be sure to check your Alka-Seltzer supply.

RECIPES

Chop Suey

Cook some of that mixed-up stuff—you know—noodles. Then go to the store and buy some suey and chop it in the noodles.

— Ray

Peanut Cookies

Get some dough out. Make it into a cookie. Put some peanuts in it and then put some sugar into it. Then bake it 33 minutes if you have a microwave, and if you have an oven, 61 minutes.

Peanut Cookies

You have to get 2 eggs. One little spoon of soaking powder. Then you mix it up. Pick up the dough and roll them into balls. Put sugar in a bowl and cinnamon and mix it up. Put the balls on the pan and cook them. Bake 10 minutes.

— Danny

Pizza

Put it in the oven.

— Dawn

Peanut Griddle

Melt some nuts. Then put some more. When it turns kinda yellowish, it's done. It tastes like candy.

— Aaron

Homemade Cookies

You put some white stuff in there. Then you crush some brown sugar. Then you stir it up. Put some cereal in it and some nutrition. Put it in a pan. Cook it 10 minutes in the oven. Eat them.

— Jeff

Cookies

Take flour, not very much; raisins to put in the cookies, a lot. Sugar, 1 cup full. Milk, a little. Stir it. Roll it out and make it into little cookies with a cookie cutter. Cook them in the oven—hot, but not a thousand degrees. Check them. They are done if they're burnt, so take them out.

— Tony

Bread

We have a wheat field at our ranch. My mom gets all the grain and flattens it out and puts it in the oven.

— Bobby

Busketti (also known as Musketti or Pusketti)

Open it with a opener-can. Dump it in a pan. Turn on the fire. Take it off the stove. Turn off the fire. Then start eating it.

— Sandra

Turkey

Mom likes to cook turkey for Thanksgiving. She gets it at the store, and she just pops it in the skillet and cooks it about 30 minutes, or 80, or 50 minutes. You can just put 30 if you want to, or 50. She does both I think. Not very hot. But she gets her stove pretty hot. She burned her fingers once. She has to take it out of the oven.

— Amy

Bologna Sandwich

Bread, bologna, chili, lettuce. Put the lettuce on the sandwich, and the bologna, and put the breads together.

— Harold

Olive Pie

Put 3 olives in the pie—chocolate or anything. Put it in the oven. Leave it 4 minutes. Then take it out and eat it.

— Terry

Biscuits

Powder, sugar, maglasses. Stir it around 'til it gets to dough. Then get a round cup and press it on the dough, and put it in the oven. The bell rings and they're done. Eat 'em.

— Amy

Chapter 8

Reading Readiness and Green Tomatoes

Brace yourself; I'm about to embark on one of my soapbox specials. I don't believe in pushing reading in kindergarten. I do believe in *lots* of reading readiness. I developed strong feelings about this while teaching first grade. I found that many first graders aren't ready to learn reading until the middle of the year. To push a child to learn reading before he has reached proper maturity is an exercise in frustration for both the child and the teacher, and it will probably result in Johnny or Joanie being totally turned off school. The average child is not ready to learn to read before age six-and-a-half.

Of course, there are some who are ready, some who figure it out on their own; perhaps from watching programs such as "Sesame Street," or following the words in a storybook while Mom reads. I would never discourage these children. Obviously, they were ready; but one still needs to be sure there are no gaps in their readiness for reading. In other words, reading is not the most important thing for a five-year-old.

This is not to imply that no reading was done in my kindergarten. Children were expected to learn to recognize their own names as quickly as possible, in order to identify their places at the tables, and to find their own lockers and to identify personal belongings. Of course, some children soon learned to read all the names at their own table; a few could read all the names in the class before the year was over. I also taught them to read the eight basic color words. They loved the challenge of "color word" worksheets. They also learned to recognize labels on things in the room and "Boys" and "Girls" on the rest room doors. But this is sight reading, "see and say," not decoding written language.

My remarks are not intended to cover all aspects of reading readiness. There are numerous books by specialists that cover the subject in depth. Burton White[3] and Arnold Gesell[4] are two authors I would especially recommend. This book is intended for enjoyment, but I must include a little on the subject since it is, or at least should be, an important part of kindergarten curriculum.

You may be asking, "What is reading readiness?" It is the set of skills a child needs to acquire, whether by plan or accident, in order to be able to learn to read. And it is risky to leave it to accident. Some of these skills are referred to elsewhere, but I will mention them again. The following are skills that need to be emphasized in kindergarten.

Visual Perception: Can Johnny or Joanie identify shapes? They need to be able to tell a triangle from a circle, otherwise how could they distinguish between an *A* and an *O*, much less distinguish one word from another? Can they pick out things that match? Things that are different? For example, can they match buttons, or squares and triangles, blocks and letters?

Auditory Perception: Can they identify familiar sounds? High and low tones? Can they identify rhyming words (words that sound alike at the end)? Beginning consonant sounds (words that begin alike)?

Memorization: Do they know the colors and the alphabet? This doesn't mean to just recite the *ABCs* or sing the *ABC* song. A lot of children can do that, but it doesn't mean a thing to them; they wouldn't know one letter from another. Knowing the *ABCs* means, for instance, looking at the headlines on the newspaper and identifying the letters by name, "That is an *E*, and this is a *T*." and so on.

Thinking Skills: Can Johnny or Joanie sort and classify objects or pictures? For instance, are they able to place animals, birds, reptiles, or fish in like groups?

At what level can they interpret pictures?

Level 1 — **Naming**. At three or four years, they should be able to identify familiar things in a picture, "boy, dog."

Level 2 — **Describing**. At about four-and-a-half or five, they might describe the action: "The boy plays with the dog. The boy has a stick."

Level 3 — **Interpreting**. At five or five-and-a-half, they should be able to identify emotions. They should be able to tell that "the boy is happy playing with his dog," rather than thinking, perhaps, that the boy is angry at his pet.

Level 4 — **Anticipating**. At age six, Johnny or Joanie should be able to predict outcomes. Example: "The boy is going to throw the stick and he wants the dog to bring it back."

These are some of the facets of reading readiness. More are mentioned in later chapters on phonics, art, and math.

* * *

I would add one thing: It is very important to allow boys more time in which to mature because they mature more slowly than girls. Studies based on boy/girl twins show that at age six the girl will be anywhere from six months to two years ahead of her brother physically, mentally, and psychologically. He will not catch up with her until about high school. Also remember that at kindergarten age, even six weeks makes an obvious difference in maturity. If your child's birthday falls so that he is barely inside the required age for school entrance, it is often wise to wait a year before letting him start, thus giving him the advantage of extra maturity.

No matter how pressing you see the need for scientists, engineers, and mathematicians, don't cheat your children out of part of their developmental childhood years by trying to rush maturity. We will get better adults for any profession if children are allowed to mature at their natural rate. Even though you can ripen green tomatoes by putting them in a sunny window, they are better if allowed to ripen naturally on the vine. But children aren't green tomatoes. Only time allows them to mature.

Chapter 9

There Are No Secrets

"My mama is going to buy us a little brother when Melissa gets big enough to go to school."

* * *

"I've had three daddies, but I don't have a daddy now. It was my second daddy that made my mommy have my little brother."

* * *

Child: "You know what? My daddy bought new carpeting for our living room and bedrooms. *Really new*! And my mama sure does like it. My daddy sure is a nice man."

Teacher: "Yes, I believe he must be a nice man. And I'll bet he's just about your best friend, too."

Child: "No, he's not. He can't be, 'cause he *lives* at our house." (Pause.) "Yes, Mama sure likes that new carpet. But you know, when we lived in Deming, my Dad drank too much beer, and he vomited on our carpet. And was Mama ever mad then!"

"There goes the trash truck. It picks up trash all over town and takes it to the dump. And that's where we get our toys."

* * *

"My mom doesn't work at the bar anymore. They threw her out."

* * *

"I think I heard my daddy say, 'I like babies that are already born.'"

* * *

"Johnny has a picture of the Beatles, and one of them is my daddy."

* * *

"My mama slept on the couch last night. I don't know why; she just slept there."

* * *

Pat: "My daddy has gone hunting today. He's going to catch a deer."

Chris: "My daddy went deer hunting, too. He always goes deer hunting."

Leslie: "My daddy *never* goes deer hunting. He always goes *snipe* hunting."

* * *

"Do you know what my daddy does after he gets off work? He just goes to the bar and gets drunk. . . . And he don't even ask my mom if he can!"

Jimmy lived on a little "ranchette," and his dad was not a rancher—no cattle. However, he frequently told about their nine pit bull dogs. One day I said, "Well, it takes a lot of food for nine big dogs. What do you feed them?"

"Oh, my dad just goes out and finds a cow and shoots it."

* * *

Little Leon waited for an opportunity to talk confidentially with the teacher. "My mom is sick. She has to take chemotherapy."

"Yes," Mrs. C. replied. "They told me in the office that she had to have surgery."

"Yeah. They cut off her boobs."

"Oh, I'm sorry."

"Well, my mom isn't. She said they were too big and heavy anyway!"

* * *

It was time for our opening quiet minute—our "moment of meditation"—and I told the children, "Now put your heads down, close your eyes, and think about something pleasant. Think a happy thought." And I set the timer for sixty seconds.

When the "ding" sounded, little Billy raised his hand. "I thought a happy thought. I thought that we're going to have a new baby at our house."

"Oh, how nice! This *is* a happy thought." I said.

"Yes, I know it is," he said, "because this morning at breakfast my mom said, 'I think I must be pregnant.' And my dad said, 'Now that's a happy thought!'"

Chapter 10

The D-Word: Dyslexia

Dyslexia is a word you hear tossed around a lot today; but what is it? Dyslexia is a problem which doctors and educators identified and began studying seriously in the late 1890s. Many theories were tested and then discarded. Since the late 1970s and 1980s, doctors and neurologists seem to have gained greater insight into the problem. While there are still many unanswered questions, we are beginning to see some progress in treatment.

First, dyslexia is a complex neurological problem that has nothing to do with a child's intelligence. It was formerly referred to as a visual-perception problem, but it has nothing to do with the person's ability to see. A person with 20/20 vision can still have a visual perception problem. In fact, the latest research seems to indicate that dyslexia is, at least in part, a problem of coordination between auditory and visual stimuli.

Dyslexia comes in many forms. The one most apparent in the classroom is left-to-right reversals as depicted in the above illustration. Another is the inability to distinguish the foreground from the background in a picture. A child's particular affliction can usually be pinpointed by a series of tests which can be administered by the school counselor or a learning-disabilities teacher. Incidentally, magazines such as *Highlights*[5] and *Sesame Street*[6] usually have puzzles that children love which are helpful for learning to cope with the different forms of dyslexia.

It should also be pointed out that dyslexia is not confined to visual problems; there are some children who have an auditory perception problem, although this seems to be much rarer than the visual perception form of the disorder. Children with this form of dyslexia may have great difficulty with phonics.[7]

Mixed Dominance

Sometimes dyslexia manifests itself in the form of clumsiness, and sometimes as hyperactivity. There is also evidence that dyslexia is associated with mixed dominance. What is mixed dominance? Consider this: if the child has a dominant right hand (more commonly known as being right-handed), but is left-footed or left-eyed, then the child has mixed dominance. Moreover, checking to see if a child has lateral dominance or mixed dominance is quite simple.

Seat him in a child-sized chair so his feet are comfortably on the floor, and then sit directly in front of him but not too close. Have in hand a cardboard tube like those that come with paper towels or toilet tissue. Select a small object across the room from the child for him to look at through your "telescope." As you hand the telescope to him try not to favor either the left or right and note which hand he uses to reach out with. Then, note to which eye he puts the "telescope." He will naturally use his dominant eye and hand. Then set the "telescope" on the floor directly in front of him and ask him to kick it. (See why I said don't sit too close?) And note which foot he uses. If it's right, right and right, or if it is left, left and left, he has lateral dominance. Some left and some right means mixed dominance. While this doesn't always signal dyslexia, it frequently does.

Since this does not pretend to be a learned dissertation on the subject, I'll leave my overly simplistic explanation at that. There are plenty of excellent books by experts available now. Except I will add, don't hit the panic button if your five-year-old reverses his *b's* and *d's*, or if your first grader reads "top" as "pot." This is so common as to be almost normal at that age. However, if a child is still doing reversals at the end of first grade, it is time to seek help. Or if he displays any symptoms of severe dyslexia, don't delay—run for help!

Some studies strongly indicate that a lot of learning disabilities can be avoided altogether simply by postponing "book learning" a little longer, and giving a child more time and opportunity to mature physically, mentally, emotionally and neurologically. After all, while learning to read is of utmost importance in our society, it is not the most important thing for a five-year-old to be doing. He will learn reading better and more quickly at six, or seven, or even eight, if he has had the opportunity to develop large muscle skills (hopping, skipping, climbing, jumping) and small muscle skills (stringing beads, coloring, using scissors, solving simple jigsaw puzzles, and such) when he is five. The proper development of muscular coordination seems to be necessary for the development of reading skills—and the avoidance of dyslexia problems. Of course, some children pick up reading on their own at an early age. If he does, don't discourage him, but do see that he develops coordination skills, also.

A Severe Case of Dyslexia

Now I want to tell you about Ronald, the first and most severely dyslexic child I ever tried to teach. This episode happened during the time when psychologists and neurologists knew considerably less about the problem, and teachers had very few resources or skills to use in helping these children. I didn't even know what the problem was, and there was no one I could turn to for help. I was teaching first grade when Ronald entered my class. He was a nice-looking child with sandy hair and blue-blue eyes which usually had a bewildered expression or showed resentment. He frequently would look straight at me, but it was as though he had pulled down a little curtain behind his eyes. Then occasionally he had a pretty good day when it seemed as though he really was with us. I was so puzzled by his behavior. There were definite indications that he was an intelligent child, but it was as though his intelligence was trapped inside and couldn't be expressed.

Ronald worked so hard, sometimes spending most of the morning on a single paper, trying to get it right, but accomplishing so little. At first I suspected it was just passive resistance; acting busy while actually doing nothing. Then I began to really notice how he went about writing his name. Each child had a name card to look at and copy as long as it was needed. But no matter how often I guided Ronald's hand while pointing to the successive letters on his card, he just couldn't get it. (I had about 35 children in my class and no aide, so my time to give individual attention was very limited.)

But if I left him alone and gave him enough time (like an hour), he could write it quite well—his way. *His way* meant that he would set the card correctly in front of his sheet of paper, and then, beginning at the *right-hand* side of his paper, he would copy from the name card, upside down and backward. When he finished, his name was correct *if* you turned the paper 180 degrees. And that was the only way he could write his name or anything else. A classic case of severe dyslexia. How tragic that we didn't know what it was or how to help!

My concern for Ronald prompted me to send several notes asking the parents to come in for a conference. But no response. Finally, I took a Sunday afternoon, picked up a friend, and drove 25 miles to the child's home out on a farm. I learned that the parents' refusal to come for a conference was because they had already made up their minds that Ronald was stupid, and they didn't need a teacher to confirm their opinion. (They had a fourth-grade daughter who was brilliant, and a younger boy who promised superiority. Poor Ronald!) All the time I was sure that

Ronald had normal, possibly superior, intelligence firmly locked inside somehow. But I couldn't convince the parents that he was not stupid and they couldn't convince me that he was. That was quite a switch. Generally it's the parent, or grandparent, trying to tell the teacher that little Johnny is at least a genius, and what the teacher sees is a little lad of average intelligence.

I wish this story had a happy ending but the family moved away before the year was over. I've often wondered, hoped and prayed, that somewhere, sometime, he had the blessing of a teacher who knew how to deal with dyslexia and was able to help him.

Other Cases

I have taught several dyslexic children since Ronald, though none so severe. With some special help and time, they have all managed in spite of the dyslexia. Most seem to develop a way to work around it. I am very much inclined to agree with those doctors, psychologists, and learning specialists who say that making sure each child has reached the needed level of maturity (not the same as age) before introducing reading would probably avoid a large percentage of dyslexia cases. Some children, like Ronald, are dyslexic regardless of maturity level and will overcome dyslexia only with special help and training. But if extra time will avoid the problem, avoidance will save the child lots of misery. Prevention is always better than a cure.

Chapter 11

More Mangling of the Language

Overheard in the classroom (you do the translation):

"My mom baked us some bikini bread."

* * *

"This is two days Pat didn't come to school. He must be playing cookie."

* * *

"Teacher, is this the day we get our credit cards?"

* * *

"Rudolph with your nose so bright, won't you drive my slaves tonight?"

* * *

"My daddy keeps a fire distinguisher in our garage."

* * *

"I need a drink. My neck is dry."

* * *

The Wise Men brought gifts to Baby Jesus—gold and myrrh and uh, uh, Frankenstein!"

* * *

My mama is in the hospital 'cause she has gobble-stones."

* * *

Teacher: "What gallops? Tell me something that gallops."
Danny: "I know! It's milk. You buy a gallop of milk!"

* * *

Teacher: "How do bears keep warm in the cold winter?"
Teddy: "They hand-grenade."

* * *

Overheard at the zoo:
Teacher: "Now, children, these animals are called llamas."
Darrin: "Well, where are the beans?"
Teacher: "The beans? What do you mean?"
Darrin: "Yes, you know—the beans—llama beans."

* * *

"Mama is decorating our house for Christmas, and she's decorating it with measles. Yeah, you know—that green stuff. And if you stand under it somebody will kiss you."

* * *

A custom observed in Mexico and the Southwest at holidays or fiestas is the piñata, a colorful papier-mache object made in the shape of an animal, a doll or a toy, and filled with candies and toys. The blindfolded youngsters strike at the suspended piñata with a stick until the piñata bursts. As one child explained, "In Mexico at Christmas they take a big stick and break a piano, and toys and candies fall out of the piano."

* * *

Teacher: "Please, Leslie, don't be touching the electrical outlet. You might get shocked."
Mike: "Yeah, and he might get persecuted, too."

* * *

Leonard: "I'm just going to get a parachute and shoot myself!" (Was he feeling adventurous—or frustrated?)

* * *

Russell: "My brother broke his leg, so the doctor put it in a plastic glass."

* * *

Discussing a picture of Eskimo children at play:

Teacher: "These children are playing a game you sometimes play. Who can tell me the name of this game?"
Jimmy: "I know. It's 'Ring Around the Collar.'"

* * *

Eddie complained, "They won't let me play with the Stinker-toys!"

* * *

Matt: " Larry, don't put that string around your arm so tight. It might cut off your selection."

* * *

Teacher: "All right children, anyone who has chewing gum should go put it in the wastebasket now."
(No response, even though some were obviously chewing gum.)
"Go ahead, get rid of your gum. I'm not going to scold you if you get rid of your gum now. But if I see you chewing gum later, I will have to scold you."
Jimmy: "What does scold mean?"
Roger: "I know. That's like if you put us in a tub of hot water!"
(A fast explanation by the teacher followed this! What a story might have been carried home; what nightmares endured if the meaning of *scold* had not been cleared up! "I will yell at you," would have been better understood.)

* * *

And what would that have made me? According to Sarah, a YELLEPHANT—that is someone who goes around yelling!

Chapter 12

Phonics Phun

In spite of the hue and cry from some quarters that English is not a phonetic language, analysis shows that English *is* about 85% phonetic, making phonics a useful and necessary tool for teaching. Thus, the experts who decided that phonics wasn't needed, wasn't even desirable, back in the 1930s, and who started the "see and say" reading method were actually trying to begin on step two of reading without first laying the foundation.

The first step in reading is the same one we all use when we come to a word we've never seen before; we decode it by analyzing the letters in their arrangement in that word. Then, after we have met up with that word a few times, we sight-read it without needing to analyze it. Without phonics, we can't figure the word out the first time. Of course, the non-phonetic words in our language we do learn "by sight." But in any event, the child who learns phonics can express himself in writing, understandably if not perfectly, at a very tender age.

In my first few years of teaching kindergarten I didn't give much time to phonics, but six years of teaching first grade showed me the importance of teaching phonics in kindergarten. I soon realized that most children actually pick up on phonics more easily before they are introduced to actual reading. This may be because to expect a child to learn the letters (two sets, upper and lower case), the sounds of the letters, then put the sounds into syllables and/or words, and read all at the same time is a real megadose of processes to assimilate simultaneously. By learning the letters and the letter sounds in kindergarten, it lessens the strain in first grade. In other words, ear training in kindergarten, eye training in first grade. Of course, not all kindergartners are going to catch on to associating a certain sound with the appropriate letter, but most do. Those who don't will at least have been introduced to the concept.

When reading to a child be sure to include little poems and Mother Goose rhymes. Children love the rhythm and rhyming, even (especially) the nonsense words: hickory dickory dock; higglety pigglety; a dillar, a dollar. They like the way these roll off the tongue, and the whole thing actually helps develop an ear for phonics. Also, alliteration, as in "Peter Piper picked a peck ..." is great for identifying beginning consonant sounds. Rhyming words carry over to learning vowel sounds and final consonants. Mother Goose has been given a bad rap the past few years, criticized for violence, as in "Ding dong bell, the pussy's in the well." Excuse me while I laugh. Just think of what is on television. I say "Up with Mother Goose!"

* * *

The first grader's phonics test was made up of a page of pictures of familiar objects. Below each picture were three consonant letters. The child was to circle the correct letter for the beginning sound for each of the pictures. In this type of test I always found that, in fairness to the child, the teacher should go over the child's paper with him because he may have incorrectly identified the picture, or perhaps called it by a different name. For instance, he may have called a hippo a pig.

Little Timmy had circled the correct letter for every picture except one. For the *cup* he had circled the *T*. I said, "Timmy, what is this picture?" And he answered, "It is a tup."

There was nothing wrong with his phonics, but a little speech therapy was in order.

We were studying the letter T, and the children were trying to think of words that began with the *T*-sounds. Mark offered this bit of information: "Toilet, that's a *T*-word. And when you go to the toilet and you don't wipe your butt, you have to go back and wipe it. And butt is a *B*-word."

* * *

As I said before, a child who has learned phonics can express himself in writing, if not perfectly, at least understandably. If his words don't look right, just read the message aloud and *listen to yourself* as you read. You will get the meaning.

An example: When my son Benny was in first grade he stopped in my room after school one afternoon while I was elsewhere. Not finding me, he left me a note:

> Dear Mother - Do't you's the pinese in your coing patas pars and if you do i em going to git prtty mad. Benny

When I was teaching first grade the teacher next door and I brewed up a supplementary worksheet for our more advanced students to do if they had time. It was dependent upon the child's ability to decode some words he hadn't had in reading and supply answers by using phonics. Each child's answers would be different because the questions were about himself, such as: "My name is _____. I am _____ years old. The color of my hair is _____. The color I like best is _____."

While this was designed for the top group, any others who wanted to try it after finishing their other work were free to do so. This activity was very revealing in that a child could either do it quite well, or not well at all. The not-at-alls, if they even attempted it, would just fill in the blanks with a jumble of letters.

After school was over for the day, Mrs. V. came to my room with Doug's paper. She said, "Can you decipher this word? I know Doug is really trying to spell something because all his other answers make sense. But I just can't figure out this one."

It read, "The food I like best is *blakidps*."

I looked at it a minute, then laughed. Can you decipher it? Excellent application of phonics for a first grader.

* * *

One phonics activity that my classes especially enjoyed took place at music time. First they learned the nursery song that says:
"Oh, a-hunting we will go, a-hunting we will go.
We'll catch a fox and put him in a box,
And then we'll let him go."

Then they made up their own verses:
"Oh, a-hunting we will go, and a-hunting we will go,
We'll catch a bear and comb his hair," or
"We'll catch a deer and wash his ear."

They thought up all kinds of verses: "Catch a raccoon and send him to the moon," or "Catch a worm and make him squirm." So, okay, extra points for originality! And the children didn't know they were learning phonics through rhyming words. They thought it was just for fun.

* * *

(In case you didn't figure it out, Doug liked black-eyed peas.)

Chapter 13

It's Only Logical

Small children have their own brand of logic, and it sometimes has some surprising twists. But it can be so basic that, as adults, it escapes us.

* * *

Scott: "Mrs. Chambers, do you know when my birthday is?"
Teacher: "Well, let me see. I have it written down here in my book. Here—it's June 4th."
Scott: "Hey, how about that! It's just the same as last year!"

* * *

On the playground as Rick was flexing his arms he said, "You ought to try this sometime. It will make you strong enough to pick up a brick. You never know when you might need a brick."

* * *

Teacher: "Andy, why did you bite Ricky?"
Andy: "Well, I didn't mean to. It was an accident."
Teacher: "How can you accidentally bite someone?"
Andy: "Well, you see, we were on the monkey bars, and I had my mouth open to say something to Scott, and Ricky pulled me off the monkey bars, and we both fell down. And my mouth was open because I was talking to Scott. And Ricky's arm just fell in my mouth!"

* * *

* * *

Teacher: "Oh, Philip, you've got your dog's picture glued upside down."

Philip: "Yeah, he likes to roll over."

* * *

I had passed out various colors of sheets of paper to the children. Bobby said, "Oh, boy, I got a green paper. That's a boy color. Red is a girl color. Blue is a boy color, and yellow is a girl color!"

(Note: Don't ask me, it's a five-year-old's logic.)

* * *

The teacher was trying to elicit the names of the three meals we eat each day. The children had remembered lunch and dinner, but no one could think of the other meal. Finally, the teacher said, "It's the meal we eat when we get up in the morning. Who knows what we call that meal?"

Jane's hand shot up and waved vigorously, "I know, I know! It's oatmeal!"

* * *

Cara still had some "baby talk" in her speech, and some of the children had trouble understanding her. Lou said, "I know why we can't understand Cara. She talks English!"

* * *

On the playground as I walked by, Ricky informed me, "I'm exercising my eyes by looking through that bush. I can see what's on the other side."

"Oh, and what do you see on the other side of the bush?"

"Well, if you walk around there you can find out."

* * *

The dress I was wearing was made of red corduroy and had a tie at the neck that ended with white angora tassels. Janice said, "Ooooh, Mrs. Chambers, you cut up Santa Claus' suit to make that dress. See? There's part of his beard."

* * *

Harry: "I'm sorry this book got marked in. My little brother did it."

Teacher: "Oh, I didn't know you had a little brother."

Harry: "Oh, yes. We've had him a lo-o-ong time, at least three or four years. He's 20 months old now."

* * *

It was late April and time for achievement tests. (Yes, even in kindergarten.) Part of the math test pertained to the child's ability to write numbers. The questions were on this order:

In the box with the apple, write the number 12.

In the box with the car, write the number 17, et cetera.

Kindergarten children often have trouble hearing the difference between numbers ending with -teen and those ending with -ty (as in four*teen* and for*ty*), so I was enunciating the numbers as distinctly as possible. We progressed to the more difficult part where the teacher would preface the directions with, "If you can," so I read, "If you can, in the box with the umbrella, write the number 84. I will repeat, eight-ty-four."

When I checked the tests I found that Robin had very carefully written:

[box with umbrella: AT 4]

* * *

Our school was in the throes of bilingual education, and all general notes and letters had to be in both English and Spanish. So I was giving a big song-and-dance about a letter from the nurse's office that was to be sent home with all children. "Now, children, this note is printed in Spanish on one side and English on the other, so if your mother doesn't read Spanish, she can just turn the paper over and read it in English."

Toni said, "But Mrs. Chambers, my mother can't read Spanish *or* English. She only reads writing!"

* * *

We were discussing a movie we had just seen teaching the

use of the telephone for emergencies. I asked, "And what would you do if you don't have a phone?" (I expected something like, "Run to a neighbor's house to call.") But Jon answered, "**Just panic!**"

* * *

At about age four, Benny and Leslie found the scissors one day and tried them out on their hair. Leslie's mom took the scissors away and told the boys they must never, never cut their hair again. Several days later when they found the scissors again they remembered that they must not cut their own hair, so they didn't; they cut Leslie's little sister's hair.

* * *

Ronald told us, "My daddy is at the graveyard to see them bury a guy in a hot rod. No-o-o-o, they aren't burying the guy *in* a hot rod. I guess he must have died of hot rod."

* * *

Going back to the "olden days" (or maybe the "dark ages") when I was in first grade, we didn't have workbooks. The teacher didn't have any kind of duplicating machine, not even one of the old gelatin "hectographs." Thus, our arithmetic seat work (we didn't even have "math" in those days, just "arithmetic") consisted of having to copy the problems which the teacher had written on the chalkboard, and then work them. It was a guaranteed method for keeping even the quickest children busy for a while.

I was normally a reasonably conscientious student, but on this particular day, by the time I got the problems copied, I decided I was too tired to work them. The whole business made me feel angry and rebellious, so I decided I would get even with the teacher. I would just show her that she was making us work too hard; I would show her by getting all the problems wrong. Which I did. Of course, that wasn't easy; I had to find the right answer first, so I could be sure *not* to put down that number. Double work, but in my mind, I thought I was getting revenge! It's all very logical—to a five-year-old!

Chapter 14

Making Little Things Count

Someone has defined a kindergarten teacher as "a smart person who knows how to make little things count."

Perhaps you are wondering how much math one can expect a kindergartner to learn. My answer is, only as much as he can internalize. Children cannot deal with abstract concepts before about eight years of age. The usual goals for math with kindergartners are these:
- Recognize and write the numerals 0 through 9.
- Have good number concepts 1 through 5.
- Learn to count at least to 30.
- Learn to count by 10s to 100.
- Identify basic geometric shapes.
- Be able to divide objects into halves.

These are things a child should be able to do by the *end* of his kindergarten year, not necessarily at the beginning.

Now, to elaborate a little. Recognizing numerals, of course, requires no explanation. Telling a 3 from a 7, for example, is an obvious need, in order to dial a telephone if nothing more.

But if number concepts 1 through 5 sounds too simple, believe me, it's as much as most fivers can handle. For a five-year-old, numbers have to be in the concrete—4 apples, 2 crayons, 1 big black dog, or whatever. Abstract math concepts

65

don't occur until the child is probably eight, possibly nine. But a five-year-old should be able to readily identify a group of three objects as 3; many can identify four objects on sight, but five objects require counting.

At five, they should also be able to conceptualize five "somethings." Beyond that, most five-year-olds tend to lose the whole concept. Not to worry though, when they are six their math horizons will expand, and again at seven, and so on. The rest will come with time, as long as someone doesn't try to push them beyond their maturity level and cause them to develop a mental block about numbers.

Many children can count to 10 when they start kindergarten; their counting always exceeds their level of understanding. Many can learn to count to 30 by rote, even if they don't understand our base-10 counting system. And they don't. Here's where counting to 100 by 10s comes in. One must be able to count by 10s in order to count to 100. So, after a child can count to 20, the next step is learning to count by 10s. And to understand what he's doing, you probably need to furnish him with 100 beans. His preference is jelly beans.

* * *

In math, as in reading and all abilities, there are always widely divergent differences. I remember a six-year-old boy who could tell you your age immediately if you told him the year you were born. Or vice versa. And this was long enough ago that some people testing him on it were born in the late 1800s, creating, of course, a two-step math process.

At the other extreme was little Gertie, a seven-year-old repeating first grade, in the room next door to mine. I dropped in for something after dismissal time one afternoon just in time to observe the teacher giving Gertie some one-on-one help with basic arithmetic:

Teacher: "Now, Gertie, how many pieces of chalk do I have in this hand?"

Gertie: "One."

Teacher: "That's right. Now, how many pieces do I have in

my other hand?"
Gertie: "One."
Teacher: "Good." (Then putting both pieces of chalk together.) "Now, how many pieces do I have here?"
Gertie: "Is it seven? Three? Five? 'leven-teen?"

* * *

This might be called "A Child's Math Logic". Five-year-old Carl was watching and wanting to be helpful while his 14-year-old brother worked on a project. Big Brother told him, "Go bring me about six nails." He felt very important being called on to help, and dutifully took big brother five nails. When he was scolded he said, "But you said 'about six,' and five *is* 'about six'."

* * *

Again, kindergarten children's number concept beyond 5, or 10 at the most, is just not there. Twenty, a hundred, a thousand or 'leventeen' — no difference. This is especially true concerning ages. I remember Michelle reporting, "Tomorrow is my mother's birthday, and she's 20. (Pause.) And my grandma is 16."

* * *

One day I overheard the following conversation:
Janice: "Today is my mother's birthday. She's four years old."
Diana: "No, Janice, that can't be. My little brother is four years old. Your mother would have to be older than that."
Janice: "Oh, no! She's four years old."
Diana: "But she has to be older than that!"
Janice: "No, she's four. Some mothers are awfully young these days."

* * *

Sooner or later during every school year some child would ask me how old I was. I usually would ask, "How old do you think I am?" One time, when I was about 30-something, this triggered the following discussion:
Lynn: "I think you must be 16 because you're bigger than my sister, and she is 15."

Carol: "Yep, I think that's right, 'cause you're not as big as my sister and she's 17."

So, the whole class agreed that Mrs. Chambers must be 16. Oh, how I loved that class!

* * *

A follow-on to the above was a discussion I overheard among girls in a junior high sewing class concerning who they thought was the youngest teacher on the faculty. At that time I happened to be the one, and I knew that, from the adult viewpoint, I looked it. But the girls decided it must either be the music teacher, who was very vivacious, or Mrs. W., who was quite petite. They just couldn't decide which. I wasn't even in the running. And, no, I didn't tell them.

* * *

I overhead this kindergarten discussion on the playground one day concerning "How old is *old*?"

Jody: "I think you're old when you're 16."

Gale: "No, you're old when you get married and have a baby."

Robbie: "No, you're not old until you have a baby girl that grows up, and then *she* has a baby. Then you're *old*."

Chris (a very observant child whose mother had been extremely ill): "Well, I don't know how old you have to be to be old, but my mother is old. I can tell by looking at her face."

Gerry (whose mother had just been selected as Mrs. Arizona of the year by the state Junior Women's Organization.): "Well, I can tell you— you're old when you're 102. And my mama is 103!"

* * *

And then there was the kindergartner who had it all figured out, "Do you know how to keep from getting old? Drop dead!"

Chapter 15

Story Translations and Transmutations

When children retell stories or nursery rhymes, they frequently insert their own interpretation. One morning a child volunteered to sing a song, and then a second child wanted to recite a nursery rhyme, followed by a third volunteer and then another. So we had nursery rhymes, riddles, folk tales and songs. This is some of what we heard.

Remember the story of the *Three Billy Goats Gruff* and the mean old troll who lived under the bridge? In Connie's version of the story it was the police who lived under the bridge. This troubled me because we don't want children to think that the policemen are their enemies. I corrected her, but wondered how she got the idea. Then it came to me:

troll = pa*trol*man = police

* * *

Any mangling of the nursery rhymes generally got corrected quickly by another child, for example:

Alex: "Little Miss Muffet sat on a tuffet, Eating her curbs away ..."

Brenda: "No, no. Not *curbs*. It's *curves*. Eating her curves away!"

Or:

Carla: "Mary had a little lamb, its feet were white as snow."
Terry: "No, ya dum-dum, not feet, *fleas*. Its *fleas* were white as snow."

* * *

David said, "I'm going to tell the story of 'The Three Pigs,' but naturally, there are really five little pigs, because there has to be a mama and a daddy pig."

* * *

Russell also liked the *Three Little Pigs* story, but in his version, the third little pig didn't buy a churn at the fair. Instead, he bought a saucer. And when he saw the wolf coming, he jumped on the saucer and slid down the hill.

* * *

In Jamie's version the little pig said, "Not by the hair of my Gemini-gin."

* * *

Danny's story, he said, was about "Little Red Robin Hood."

* * *

Amy sang "Ten Little Indians" for us, a song we use a lot because it is a challenge for the development of hand coordination, and children like the challenge. Amy's coordination wasn't quite achieved yet, and at the end of "10 little Indian boys" I heard her say, "Oops, 11! I keep coming out with 11!"

* * *

At the end of *This Little Piggy Went To Market*, Ken added, "I know why one little pig cried 'wee-wee-wee' all the way home. He had to go to the bathroom."

* * *

Kris and Pat took the story of *Little Red Riding Hood* quite seriously. After I had read it one morning I noticed them over by the window in a deep discussion. Then they came to me with, "We think *Little Red Riding Hood* was just plain dumb. She could have turned around and run back home!"

* * *

Cindy had her own version of *The Three Bears* with a different twist, and she told it very well. It concluded thus:

"When the three bears came home they knew someone had been in their house. Papa Bear said, 'Who's been drinking my beer?' Mama Bear said, 'Who's been eating my beans?' And Baby Bear said, 'Who's been playing my records?'

And Goldilocks went, 'Hic! Pu-u-ut! Cha-cha-cha!'"

* * *

Then Keith made this contribution. Perhaps you have heard it; I hadn't. He recited it with great dramatization:

"Birdie, birdie, in the sky,
Why'd you do that in my eye?
But I won't fret and I won't cry;
I just thank God that cows can't fly!"

Chapter 16

Do-Re-Mi-I-E-I-O"

Small children and music just naturally go together. Even a toddler will try to imitate the singing he hears and will often try to dance when hearing music with a good rhythm. Music is used in kindergarten for singing, for fun, and to help children develop coordination and a sense of rhythm. It is also used for ear training, to teach counting and rhyming words, and to reinforce things taught in other areas.

I always found that kindergartners' favorites were action songs. They are challenged both by the words and the coordination and timing of the actions. As the year progressed they were able to do well on songs that required very accurate timing for the actions; and they loved it.

Children also love the rhythm band instruments. They soon learn to maintain the rhythm and stay on the beat; at least most of them. Those who have difficulty usually can stay on the beat if the teacher can maintain eye contact with them. But if their eyes wander, so does the attention and they're off the beat again.

In addition to action songs, the children love action music: skipping, marching, and any music they can move to. One particular day, the children paraded around the room as I played songs about various zoo animals. Rather than singing, they were to imitate the animals of each song. Each one was acted out appropriately: the kangaroo hopped, the elephant gal-lumped, et cetera. When I played the monkey song I expected them to either start jumping around or to start "climbing." But no, they all stopped dead in their tracks and started scratching fleas!

* * *

In past years, publishers of children's music books seemed to have had the opinion that because children have light, higher-pitched speaking voices, they could sing only in a high range. Not so. At the beginning of kindergarten most children will have a singing range between middle C and A; a few up to C. Above that, they just stay on their top note. When I began teaching kindergarten the only music books available to me had the songs all written so high they were unsingable to most children and adults. (I'm an alto, so it was a real problem for me.) I used two methods to solve the problem. I don't play by ear, and I can't transpose on sight. So I would take the book home and rewrite the music in a lower key, checking it against my piano.

The other method was to sing the song without the piano in my range and teach the children the words. Then I would play it as it was written in the book and depend on the one very musically talented child, Linda, to lead in singing. The other children followed her. She didn't realize she was helping teach the class!

Fortunately, about that time the compilers of children's songbooks began to realize that very few children can sing so high, and they began to rewrite the music within a reasonable range.

I learned by experience that usually at the beginning of kindergarten something between 50% and 75% of the children cannot carry a tune. Those who have had access to a record or tape player and children who have been exposed to children's songs regularly, as in Sunday school, will usually be among those who can carry a tune. In school you have music every day if possible, and before the year is over at least 75% will be able to carry a tune, within the limits of their singing range. But never tell a child that he can't sing. Most will learn to carry a tune in due time if they are encouraged to sing.

* * *

When words of a song are unfamiliar to a child he will interpret them according to words he has heard. Hence, I overheard Johnny's version of "Rhinestone Cowboy"—it was "Ridin' Stoned Cowboy."

* * *

Kathleen, like all children, didn't always get the words right. When she was perhaps two years old I heard her in the kitchen trying to sing. She didn't seem pleased with the way her song was going. I listened and heard a rather tuneless, "Donald Duck had a worm, Donald Duck had a worm ..." She looked very puzzled by the way it came out, but still she tried again ... "Donald Duck had a worm, Donald Duck had a worm..." still very puzzled. I wondered what she was trying to sing, what was on her mind? Then suddenly she got it, and sang it, at least her version, perfectly well: "Old Duck Donald had a worm, E-I-E-I-O."

* * *

The music teacher had been teaching the action song, "I'm a Little Teapot[8]," which children enjoy very much. But Mrs. B. had second thoughts when she heard one child, from a large, very poor family, whose inadequate house lacked basic plumbing, singing the song as he understood it: "I'm a little *pee pot*." And as she thought through the words of the song,
 "I'm a little teapot short and stout,
 Here is my handle, here is my spout.
 When I get all steamed up, then I shout,
 'Just tip me over and pour me out!'"

Mrs. B. had a clear picture of the child's interpretation!

* * *

* * *

Mrs. H. and Mrs. B. always brought their first-grade classes to my room so we could "music" together. On this day we told the children to close their eyes and listen to the record, and try to see in their minds what the music was telling them. The record was John Philip Sousa's "Stars and Stripes Forever." When it was finished, Mrs. H. asked, "Now, who would like to tell us what they saw?"

One of her students raised his hand and said, "I heard a band playing."

One of mine said, "I saw a parade!"

At that moment all of Mrs. B.'s children jumped up, ran to the windows and looked out.

Oh, well...

Chapter 17

Nature Lessons from Children

Nature—facts of life—if children don't like your explanation, they will give you their own.

* * *

Peggy: "We saw a snake that was half bull snake and half rattlesnake. And then we saw another that was half bull snake and half English."

* * *

Dixie: "We had a little black-and-white rooster that laid brown eggs. But he's dead now. (Pause) Daddy shot him 'cause he talked too much."

* * *

The conversation was about kittens. Danny told us, "Before they're born their eyes are closed. They don't know where they're going."

* * *

Jeff: "My dog isn't ever going to have any more babies. And, Teacher, do you know why? Because we had the eggs took out!"

* * *

Two brothers, ages six and eight, were telling me their big news:

Bill: "Our daddy killed a snake, and it was a bull snake."

Tim: "No, it wasn't a bull snake!"
Bill: "Yes, it *WAS* a bull snake."
Tim: *"NO, IT WAS NOT!"* (And on and on…)

Finally, I interrupted the argument and asked, "Tim, how do you know it wasn't a bull snake? There are lots of bull snakes around here. How can you be so sure?"

Tim: "But it *wasn't* a bull snake. It was a mother snake! When Daddy killed it we found baby snakes inside!"

* * *

Annette: "Our mother cat had kittens because he's a female. And now his kittens are females. And Skippy is our mother dog, and he's a female. And he had puppies, and now all his puppies are males!"

* * *

The science lesson centered on the protective coverings of various kinds of animals. One child told us, "Fish have scales." Another one added, "Birds have feathers." Then they seemed to be stumped, so I asked, "What do dogs have?" Marcia answered, "I know. Fleas!"

* * *

Freddie was explaining his drawing to the class:

"This is a person…and the others are people who are still in the eggs."

* * *

* * *

Gene: "There are seven chickens. They will get seven eggs."
Morgan: "No, only six, because one chicken is a rooster."
Gerry: "Yeah. Roosters don't lay eggs."
Gene: "Then why would a farmer want a rooster?"
Morgan: "Because they give the hens—uh, they give the hens…uh…"
Gerry: "Extra protein! They give the hens extra protein!"

Chapter 18

The Field Trip that Wasn't

Today was to be the *big day* for the kindergartners: we were going for a train ride! Everyone had to be at school fifteen minutes early with a sack lunch (be sure your name was on it), so we could load onto a school bus and go to Tucson. There we would catch the Amtrak back to Benson, where our bus would be waiting for us. We would eat our lunch in the Benson park before returning by bus to Willcox, arriving just in time for afternoon dismissal, and for many, another bus ride home. (Amtrack comes through Willcox but refuses to stop here— not even once a year to accommodate the 80 passengers on a kindergarten field trip.)

Everything was going fine as we rolled merrily down I-10. Checking our watches we saw that, although it was a rather tight schedule, we would reach the station in Tucson with just a comfortable amount of time to spare. Then at about 9:30— Pow! Bang! Clank! Clank! The bus engine came to a sudden, violent death as black smoke boiled out from under the hood. The bus driver guided the powerless bus out of the traffic lane and onto the shoulder as far as possible. And there we sat, 20 miles from Tucson, 65 miles from Willcox. The bus driver raised the hood

79

and peered under, but of course, it was a hopeless case—D.O.A.

This was before cellular phones, or at least before they came into widespread use, so we had no way to get help. Thus, some 20 adults—two teachers, an aide, the bus driver, and parent volunteers—and about 60 kindergartners found themselves stranded on the major east-west freeway crossing southern Arizona. We hoped for a highway patrol car, but none came.

We flagged down a pickup and asked the driver to please, when he got to Tucson, call the school in Willcox and tell them we were in trouble. He had a CB, but it was of no use at that distance and with a mountain range in between. As a backup measure, we flagged two other vehicles with the same request, giving them the school number and offering to pay them for the call. They assured us they would, but none of them ever called.

So we sat, and sat, and sat. Every time a big semi-truck went past, the air currents would cause the bus to rock. It was scary! And we waited. Ten o'clock . . . 10:30 . . . we got a glimpse of Amtrak gliding down the rails a few miles away across the desert. There we sat. Oh well, we thought, when our rescue bus gets here, we'll take the kids to visit the zoo instead. That was on the agenda for the near future anyway.

Amazingly, the children sat quietly chatting with each other, occasionally asking an adult, "When ..." Still we sat and waited. Eleven o'clock . . . 11:30 . . . forget the zoo . . . not enough time for that even if we were there right now.

Then we began to hear, "I'm hungry," so we told the children, "Yes, you may eat your lunch. Be sure to put any scraps or papers back in your sack. No litterbugs allowed!" Soon we heard, "I'm thirsty." But the answer to that was "No," even though we had a five-gallon cooler of lemonade. We knew what would come next if they were allowed drinks.

Finally, at about 12:30 a pickup stopped. It was the bus supervisor from the Vail school, which lies a few miles from the freeway. He was horrified to find that a busload of children had been stranded on the freeway for 3 hours. He radioed to his school for a bus to be sent over to pick us up and take us to Vail, and also, for someone to put in a call to the school superintendent in Willcox. We felt that our Good Samaritan had finally come! He directed that the bus come to the nearest point on an access road, rather than having children change buses on the freeway. Thus, we "snaked" the children across 200 yards of desert to the rescue bus.

At Vail Elementary School we were treated royally. They didn't realize that our children had their lunch already, and were going to give them milk and whatever else was available in their cafeteria. We said, "No, they've had their lunches, but they are thirsty. Just show them the water fountains ... and the way to the toilets!"

Then their teachers said, "You've been cooped up on the bus with 60 kids for three hours? Let them go to the playground; we'll watch them. You go into the lounge and help yourself to the coffee or sodas." We gladly accepted their offer.

In about an hour the Willcox High School activity bus, usually reserved for sports teams, arrived for us. We made it safely back to Willcox in style; the activity bus had Greyhound bus type seats. Back home the good ol' yellow school buses were waiting for our arrival so they could claim their riders and take them home.

To me, the most remarkable, even amazing part of the whole episode, the thing that made me proud, I mean *really* proud of our children was this: As we sat there with the traffic whizzing past, not one child panicked, not one child cried, there was no squabbling, and there were no wet pants. What a wonderful bunch of kids! What more could you ask for?

Chapter 19

Amateurs' Analysis of Amtrak

Arranging for the train trip from Tucson to Benson hadn't been easy, so we weren't going to let a broken-down bus stop us. The following week we rescheduled the trip, and it went smoothly. The children were excited and had plenty to say about the trip.

A homework assignment always followed a field trip. Each child was to engage a "secretary" (a parent or some other adult) to write down what the child thought about the trip. Most parents were very cooperative secretaries. The following comments are taken from reports about train ride field trips that took place over several years. You may be surprised by the things that impressed the children most.

* * *

"We got on a train, then we got it going."

* * *

"We went six miles. The train went slow at first. It went slow seven times, and then it went fast. There was hot water in the railings."

"The train started slow— s-l-o-w—*s-l-o-w*, like an old dog. Then it went *fast!*"

"We went up some steps ten feet high! We sat down — then we went to this door. We pushed a button and got caught in a place between two cars. We stepped between two cars. We saw where the beds were. Then we saw where the sink was. The toilet was right below the sink. They had the same kind of beds as the sink. You pull it down."

* * *

"It was real hot where they cooked the lunch. The train sounded like it was going to fall apart!"

* * *

"The train was like a two-story house. And it wiggled while it was going."

* * *

"We seen all them little rooms in the other cars. There was bunk beds and flat beds. There was a chair bathroom—a little bitty bathroom, and the sink folded down from the wall."

* * *

"We said "Hi" to the man driving the train. We walked to another train (car), and we had to be careful or it might hook off."

* * *

"We speeded up. Then we went on a road where there was just a road and *not a thing* under it! The scariest part was when we walked between the cars, when the wind was coming through, and nothing was holding the cars together but *pure magnets*!"

* * *

"We saw lots of train wheels. I guess those were the spare wheels. I told my mommy, 'Hey, we're moving, and we aren't on the tracks!' 'cause I couldn't see the tracks. When we looked out the window we could see the train engine as we went around the curve."

* * *

"A man with a mustache with curls on the end helped me up the steps. I liked the bathroom the best of the train because they had soft things on the toilet so when you went over a bump it wouldn't hurt your rear end!"

* * *

* * *

"There was an upstairs that was about a hundred feet up."

* * *

"We went through the doors and it was real shaky and movey. You could see the railroad tracks through the cracks."

* * *

"Looked out the windows and saw a cave—Colossal Cave, and an old castle, houses, and a little shack."

* * *

"We were real high up so we could see a hundred miles!"

* * *

"We had to cross these little metal floors that were moving. Sometimes you could see both the front of the train and the back of the train."

* * *

"When you were walking it kinda felt like you were walking when the world was turning around."

* * *

"We went slow and we stopped by the cement on the side of the track to get gas."

* * *

"I liked the buttons best. They had buttons on *everything*! The seats and the trays had yellow buttons. And a black button to flush the toilet."

* * *

"Got on the bus and went back to school, and came home. Now I am home. Now we are writing it down. Write that down, Mom. That's all!"

Chapter 20

A is for Art

I love kindergartners' art. A child can experiment at the easel and blob a lot of happy colors on a sheet of paper, or even mix them up so his colors aren't so happy, and still finish with a "picture" that may be pleasing to look at. And I think it is wonderful. It also reveals his level of maturity.

In evaluating children's art, the first consideration is the age of the artist. The drawing ability of young children changes rapidly as they go through various levels of maturity. Actually, the child's maturity level, which may or may not be the same as his chronological age, can be assessed quite accurately from the way he draws a person. In fact, there is a standardized test, the Draw-A-Man Test[9] developed by Florence Goodenough, that can be very useful in determining a child's developmental level.

So what can we expect at different ages? The first marks a child can make with a pencil or crayon will be vertical ones; a two-year-old will do this. It will be a while before a horizontal line is achieved. Usually the child will be about five-and-a-half before he can make a diagonal line by himself. All of this will be apparent in his attempts at drawing and writing. Note the lopsided roofs on his houses and the lopsided A*s* when he attempts to write. The letter K is very difficult for children to master because of the diagonal lines. Their Xs will look more like plus marks. Also, at this age, their circles will be started at the bottom.

When it comes to drawing, a three-year-old's man may be a balloon with a leg, or two, maybe; and an eye, or two, maybe. At four years there will be some improvement, but even some five-year-olds are still at this level. Some children will draw stick figures, but most draw balloons. By five-and-a-half or six years, a child usually can draw a reasonably well-proportioned figure and include legs, arms, face and hair. Some will include fingers and/or toes, not necessarily the correct number, but they seldom forget to add the belly button! Some will show indications of clothing. At six-and-a-half, the child should be able to do all of this.

3 or 4 years   4 or 5 years   6 or 6 1/2 years

When the assignment was to draw a man, little Bill's figure was really quite good, well proportioned, even showing action, but it wore no clothes. And there was no doubt about it; it *was* a man! I made no comment, but Bill volunteered, "This is my daddy. He's a streaker."

* * *

A child's artwork reveals certain aspects of his personality. In fact, very often there is something about a child's pictures that actually look like the child. Many times I have been able to guess who drew an unlabeled picture because it looked like the child. And certainly the child's way of thinking is revealed.

* * *

Incidentally, I found that when a child shows his artwork, one should never say, "What is it?"

Instead you say, "Tell me about your picture." If it is his attempt at drawing something, he will tell you. If he was just having fun using his crayons, he will also let you know that, too. Sometimes the child is experimenting with repeating a pattern or making a design, although he probably wouldn't say it that way. Whatever the attempt, we don't criticize. And in coloring, a five-year-old cannot always stay inside the lines. Just think *maturity level*.

* * *

I remember Catarina, a little Hispanic girl with some learning difficulties. I watched as she was painting at the easel—first, the usual house with a tree beside it. Then, beginning near the bottom of the sheet she made a circle. Inside the circle she put two dots side by side, and above that a short horizontal line. Above the circle she added a vertical rectangle. I wondered what she was making: it was definitely not the usual stereotyped thing. Then to my surprise she added two legs sticking up from the rectangle. Was this a visual perception problem? So I asked her to tell me about her picture. She looked at me like, "What's the matter with you?" and said, "The little girl is standing on her head!"

So-o-o-oo, well, okay!

* * *

Another interesting aspect of the children's art is their choice of colors. Happy children tend to select happy colors, and yellow is the happiest of all. But I always felt concern if a child constantly chose only black or purple as this often indicates a sad or depressed child.

However, before setting the diagnosis in concrete, check all the possibilities. I recall Mary, who used only purple in her drawings. Her concerned teacher showed some of Mary's papers to the counselor, and it was arranged for her to have a chat with

Mary. The counselor was unable to pick up on any underlying sadness or depression, so she finally asked Mary about her drawings and why she always used only purple. Mary replied, "Because I lost my other crayons. I only have purple."

In some kindergarten classes, children share crayons from a large tray. I preferred that each child have his own box. First, I felt that it helped them learn to be responsible for their own belongings, and second, it helped them learn the difference between *mine* and *thine*.

Kindergarten art is not always crayons or paint and paper. Sometimes it is cut-and-paste, modeling clay, stitchery, or something else depending on the creative ingenuity of the teacher or the children. Sometimes I had the children each bring a few small cardboard boxes from which each child created a "something," usually an animal, but sometimes it was a castle or a car or a doll cradle. Paint, glue, wheels, yarn, and imagination made it lots of fun.

We always did a stitchery project using burlap and yarn, good for both imagination and coordination. Boys and girls enjoyed this equally. But what I overheard little John tell himself while stitching away was, "I *should* be going to medical school or at least first grade!"

Cut-and-paste isn't as simple as it sounds. Teaching children how to use paste wasn't always easy. Some children just couldn't understand that the pieces to be pasted had to be turned over and paste applied to the back side. They were sure that the trick was to put enough paste on top to weigh it down into place. And then there were always the paste eaters. The paste didn't hurt the child, but it was hard on the paste supply. However, I found a solution. Each time I got a large, new jar of paste, I would take it home, dump the paste into a mixing bowl, and stir in *blue* food coloring. Then, back into the jar and back to school. I would suggest to the children that *foods are never blue*, so it would be best not to taste the paste. It worked! Later, the advent of white "school glues" eliminated the use of paste and took care of this problem.

***

The big rodeo of the year was fast approaching, so a little western art was in order. I gave the children precut shapes consisting of three pear-shaped pieces in graduated sizes. These were to be assembled in overlapping fashion to make the body, neck, and head of a horse. Then there were four legs, with knees somewhat bent, to be attached. Next the child could add tail, eyes, ears, mane, and any other details with crayon. I had matching pieces of felt to demonstrate at the flannel board the various poses their horses might take. With these pieces the horse could be made to face either left or right. He could be walking, bucking or drinking, according to how he was assembled. Actually, almost any way they were put together, the result made a recognizable horse. Only a few of the least mature children might create something resembling an explosion in a glue factory.

I had finished my demonstration at the flannel board and left the last horse there. He didn't look quite right; however, I didn't expect a photographic likeness to an equine creature. But little Brian, who was extremely talented in drawing and whose specialty was horses, spoke up very politely, almost meekly, "Mrs. Chambers, your horse would look better if you turned his back legs the other way."

Sure enough, I had his back legs bending the wrong way. Thereafter, I was careful to remember that a horse's front and back knees bend in opposite directions!

Then there is the matter of scissors. Many five-year-olds can use scissors when beginning kindergarten, or develop the coordination to do so without undue difficulty. However, there are always a few who have problems. There are double-handled training scissors that are useful in teaching this skill. Also, for the left-handers, there are left-handed scissors, even for kindergartners. So, if you have a preschooler, be sure he has a pair of good, round-nosed scissors and some old magazines, and a wastebasket for scraps. Note that I said *good*. Leave the cheapies for an older child to cope with; beginners need good scissors.

I began this by saying that kindergarten art is wonderful. It is, but I always feel rather sad when these children lose their spontaneity and begin to draw, day after day, the same little square house with a hip roof, one door, and two windows. I would love to see them keep their uninhibited enthusiasm and individualism in their artwork, and see an ever-increasing ability to express their ideas in art.

Chapter 21

The View from 45 Inches

Forty-five inches is the average height of kindergartners and they frequently have a different view of things than adults, and not just because they are two or three feet shorter than we are. Their point of view is not only different, but often it's a fresher view than we have. For instance:

It must have been February because our *Weekly Reader*[1] had a picture and story about George Washington in it. As the children looked at his picture I heard Brenda say, "O-oo-oh, he wears his hair in the cutest flip!" And Ricky said, "Looks to me like he has shaving cream on his head!"

* * *

Judy had told me how "mean" her baby brother was, and added, "But *I* was a good baby!" The next day I asked her, "Well Judy, is your little brother being mean today?"

Judy: "No, he's a good baby. But you have to be good to babies. 'Cause if you leave him lying on the bed while you go to get a blanket, he'll fall off on his little head, and then he'll cry a lot."

Teacher: "Maybe you need another little brother. Would you like that?"

Judy: "Oh, no. They might be twins. And I wouldn't want twins. You know why? 'Cause they both would have to be fed at the same time, and I don't think I could do that."

Teacher: "Well, lots of mothers have twins. Do you suppose they feed one and then put him to bed, then feed the other one? Or do you suppose they give this one a bite, and then the other one, then this one, and then the other?"

Judy: "Well, if *I* had twins, I'd feed them one at a time (pause) and then I'd change their diapers one at a time!"

* * *

Lynn informed me, "Mrs. Chambers, if you want me to write this in *real-people* writing, you're just out of luck. I can't write *real-people* writing."

* * *

We had taken a walking field trip after a rain on the previous night. One child remarked, "Hey, today we have to walk *on* the water!"

And after our return another child complained loudly, "It sure was a long ways to walk. Why, that's farther than Arkansas!"

* * *

A few weeks into first grade, Russ dropped into my room after school one day. He spoke to me, then walked around the room, looking at the bulletin boards, furniture arrangement, and other things. I was feeling flattered that he thought enough of his kindergarten teacher to come back to visit. But my ego trip was short-lived. After inspecting the room he left with this parting remark, "I just wanted to see if this room was as weird as ever!"

* * *

Small Anglo children (and many adults) have very erroneous ideas about Native Americans, thanks largely to movies and TV. No amount of explaining that Native Americans are people just like us could erase that image, so Mrs. D. and I worked out arrangements with the kindergarten teachers on San Carlos Apache Reservation to take our classes there to visit.

We visited their classroom and cafeteria, had a sack lunch picnic with the Apache children, and then the children lined up to go to the playground, each of our children with a partner from our host school. As we walked along, little Chris said to me, "Mrs. Chambers, I haven't seen a single Indian yet."

I said, "Chris, who do you think you're holding hands with?"

"I mean, I haven't seen a single Apache."

"Chris, your new friend, your partner right now, is an Apache."

"Well, what I mean is that I haven't seen a bad Indian — or one with feathers!"

* * *

We had an ailing cow which required a trip to the veterinarian at a neighboring town. Benny was about four years old at the time, so his father Clell asked Benny if, instead of going to the babysitter, he would like to go with him to take the cow to see "the nice cow doctor." Benny was excited about the trip, and on the way the conversation, of course, was about the "cow doctor."

When they arrived, Clell noticed that Benny's enthusiasm faded quickly, and he was unusually quiet on the way home. Finally, with his lip quivering, he said, "Daddy, you said we would see a cow doctor. That wasn't a cow doctor. That was just a man!"

* * *

On another occasion Clell was making a purchase in the hardware store and was only vaguely aware that a young woman with a child in tow had entered the store and were standing nearby. He soon felt a tug on the hem of his jacket. Looking down he saw the child beaming up at him and saying, "I know who you are. You belong to Mrs. Chambers!"

* * *

In spite of my original college major in home economics, I have always considered cooking an evil necessity. Only on rare occasions did I have a genuine urge to cook. However, my mother liked to cook, and whenever she came I usually turned the kitchen over to her. My son Benny was especially fond of the cinnamon rolls Grandmother baked. Likewise, whenever he went to his Grandma Chambers' house, his usual greeting was, "Grandma, let's make cinnamon rolls." And she always complied.

One Saturday I decided I would bake cinnamon rolls. I was in the midst of the process when Benny came through the kitchen. He stopped and stared in amazement for a moment, then said, "You're making cinnamon rolls? I thought only grandmothers could make cinnamon rolls!"

Chapter 22

Aides and Anna's Bananas

The concept of classroom aides for teachers is a wonderful one that should have been thought of long ago. I could certainly have used an aide when I was coping with kindergartens or first grades of 35 or more students. I believe it was in 1974 when our school system began hiring full-time aides, usually one or two per grade level. I might have been just a little biased, but I always felt that my fellow kindergarten teachers and I were very fortunate; we got the very best aides in the system.

Later, our school set up a system where parents were encouraged to volunteer as aides on a regular schedule of one half-day per week. This generally worked out quite well. I usually had a volunteer for every day of the week for both morning and afternoon classes. One year I had a mother, Linda, who volunteered for *every* afternoon, five days a week for the entire year. What a blessing she was!

I gratefully recall these volunteers for whom it was a double benefit. It gave them a better understanding of what can be reasonably expected from a five-year-old and of their own child's individual needs, while adding greatly to the effectiveness of classroom teaching.

I especially remember Jackie, Esther, Helen, and Betty, who volunteered full-time for anywhere from several weeks to a few years, and who didn't even have children in school. What wonderful, generous people!

Also, at one point in connection with a class at the high school we had high school student aides for a few years. This met with varying degrees of success, depending on the student's reliability, as well as the aptitude and interest the student had in working with small children. Of all these young volunteers, the one I always remember with a smile is Anna. I'm not sure she was particularly enamored with small children; it seemed to be more that she got an ego boost from being almost-a-teacher.

I found Anna to be totally reliable and likeable, and at times somewhat amusing. She was precise in her manner of speaking, sometimes sounding almost like a little old granny. Sometimes I could have sworn she was older than I! And again, she could be very childlike. She was bright in some areas, and in others she had definite difficulties. I often wondered if she had some variety of dyslexia or if it was simply an eye-hand coordination problem.

Anna loved to help with the snack preparation and serving. However, there were some things she just couldn't handle. For example, if the snack were oranges, the serving would be half an orange, with seconds for those who wanted more. But we learned not to let Anna cut the oranges, as she simply could not get the two parts anywhere near equal. It was the same with anything that required bisecting. If the task was to cut the cake, baked in a standard 9 x 13 pan, to serve 24 students—no way could she figure out how to cut that into six pieces across the length and four across the width. Her result would be three-inch slabs of cake for some children and one-inch slivers for others.

But what I remember most is what I think of as "Anna's Banana Caper." It was necessary for me to leave school for a short period that morning, and I was leaving my class in the care of Judy, our regular aide, with Ellen, the other kindergarten teacher, in charge of both classes. A door between our classrooms made it all very easy, and the snacks for both classes were prepared together. As I started to leave, there was Anna taking it upon herself to cut the large bananas in half. Only she was attempting to cut them lengthwise as you would for a banana split.

As I walked past I said, "It would be easier if you cut them the other way." It crossed my mind to tip off Ellen to the problem, then I thought, "No, Ellen and Judy can handle this one," and I went on my way.

It was lunchtime when I returned. The morning class was gone, Anna had returned to the high school, and in my classroom I found Judy and Ellen doubled over with laughter. Anna had misunderstood my suggestion, and rather than cutting the bananas across, she had laid each one on its side, and slicing it lengthwise, cut it so each child got either a sort of half-moon shaped piece, or else a piece which consisted of the two ends connected mostly by a strip of peel.

When the children came in from recess and saw these strangely shaped snacks at their places their reaction was, "What is this?" One child who had received a half-moon portion, after he had eaten the fruit, brought the peel, intact and carried carefully in his cupped hands, and asked Ellen, "Teacher, may I take this home? I *think* my mother wants to make something out of it."

It was Anna's problem with getting two parts equal that prompted me to set up a combination math-snack lesson whereby pairs of children divided Twinkies into halves. I wondered if five-year-olds could do something that Anna couldn't do. They could.

Chapter 23

Git Along, Little Dogies

"What do cowboys do?" I asked my kindergartners. "Shoot Indians," was the instant reply. "No way," I said, "cowboys don't shoot anybody."

When the Willcox area was almost exclusively ranching, every child knew that a cowboy's life was hard work—riding the pastures, looking for animals needing medical attention, building or repairing fences, a yearly roundup, branding and de-horning calves, separating animals to go to the market, and a thousand other chores—with very little time for strumming on a guitar and singing love songs. Never, never shooting Indians. In fact, the cowboy might himself be an Indian.

But with the intrusion of large-scale farming into this area in the late 1950s, not to mention the false picture given by the movies, we found more and more children knew nothing of what ranching was all about—even at Willcox, the town that once was dubbed the "Range Cattle Capital of America." Consequently, I began trying each year to arrange a field trip to one or another of the nearby ranches to give the children an opportunity to learn about ranching. These excerpts from the children's "homework" will contain some variations reflecting methods used at different ranches. The first one is by a ranch child who was familiar with the various processes and who told it well.

* * *

"First they put the calf in the squeeze chute. Then they dehorned him and cut a piece out of his ear so they could tell whose calf it was. Then they branded him 'G-Bar'. And they cut the testicles off the bull. Then they did another one the old way—they laid it out on the ground and dehorned it. It was a steer, and they branded it. They showed us how to shoe a horse, and they showed us how they fed a calf out of a bucket with a nipple on it because the mamma didn't have any milk."

* * *

"We went over and watched through the fence. They showed us branding. Mommy, I will write this brand for you. It is a *W*, and they put lines on it and call it a *Flying W*. They branded this little calf about two days old. Mommy, don't write this down, but if I was them, I'd wait about a month, 'cause he was little. They gived him a shot like we have, to keep them from getting black leg. And they cut their ears different."

* * *

"They put ink in their ears. I got a piece of ear. Their ears were clean too."

(Note: Some ranchers tattoo a number in each calf's ear as a method by which they can keep a record of each individual animal. Others may ear-tag the animals.)

* * *

"We saw a steer. It wasn't a bull because it had short horns. They cut a thing out back behind their hip…something it didn't need anyway. They branded an *E* and a *U* on them."

* * *

"They cut off the calf's nursey-nursey."

* * *

"One cowboy could rope better than the others. I think he had a better rope."

* * *

* * *

"The man got on his horse. Boy, did he go fast through the corral! One man said, 'Don't you wish you were a calf so you could be branded?' And us kids all said, 'Oh, no!'"

* * *

"The baby cows ran to their moms so they could lick their 'ouchies'. They gave them shots like I got so I could go to school.

"We saw a baby calf roped, and they tied it to a fence so we could pet it. We saw them brand a calf. They branded them, cutted a piece of their ear, and gave them shots. They didn't give them pills. Then they letted them go. We got to see them put a shoe on a horse, and I told them that I knew how to do all that stuff."

* * *

"Saw some spotted bulls. They had long horns. Some of the horns went forward, and some went up. They used pliers to cut off the horns of the cows."

* * *

"Last night a daddy cow that was spotted had a baby."

* * *

"They squeezed his milkers to get the milk out."

* * *

One squeamish child said, "When they cut the horns off I didn't want to look because I thought I might get sick—and when they put the brand on I didn't look. I didn't have any fun." (This was a very unusual reaction.)

* * *

"The man branded a calf in a kind of cow-machine. I forget what they call it. They put the cow in a thing what it just walks into."

* * *

"They squeezed the cow's neck with a gun—not the shooting kind." (A little confusion here between *chute* and *shoot*.)

* * *

***

"I saw a fire, and they were doing that—I forgot what it was called—making words on a cow."

***

"It was smelly out there. The other kids smelled something, but I kept my nose plugged."

***

"The first cow cried when they touched him with the hot iron. The second cow didn't. He was a good cow. That hot thing just mashed the hair down and made a design."

***

"I saw them dig the food out of the wide, wide, deep hole (ensilage pit). That stuff smelled like pickles."

***

"We got to watch them make a salad for the cows. They don't get lettuce, of course; they get milo and cotton seeds and make some salad for them."

***

"He had a tractor and it picked up the hay, and it turned into cow food hay. He put it in the dish and the cows ate it."

***

"They put a shot in them; the cattle didn't talk. The cow was very brave of the branding."

***

"We went to this place and these people were branding. It was OK, but my daddy does it better."

***

"They put tags on the ears of the cows with a bottle opener thing. It left like earrings with a number on it."

***

"When the babies are little, they drink from their mother's tummies, and when they are a lot bigger their mothers just kick 'em away cause they gots teeth and have to eat hay. When the bulls—boy cows—get kicked away, the mother says 'Moo, moo,' and that means to go eat hay. Females are girl cows, and when it's a bull it's a boy cow—mostly."

* * *

"We went to Mr. Chambers' ranch. They were branding, and tied their feet with a piggy string. They put the branding sticks in fire. Then they put them on the cows. It stunk! I told you it was gross. They put them in a cage with their mother, and they run right to their mother. The mother said in cow language, 'It will be all right.' Then she licked it right across the mark. They did a whole bunch of cows with an *A L L*."

(Note: A pigging, or piggy, string is a small rope.)

"The brand that they writed on the cows was *A L L*. After they burned them they painted the brand with black paint. Then they gave them a shot and then untied his feet. Then they brought it to the mother cow. The little cows cried, 'Blah, Blah.' But when they went to their mommies they were okay. One of the little cows smiled at me by the fence."

* * *

"I got to climb up on the fence and look at the baby cows. Then I went over and stood by Mrs. Chambers' husband. The bull was the daddy. The milking cow was the mamma. We standed on a wooden fence to watch the cows go out."

* * *

You have probably noticed an almost total lack of squeamishness in the children's comments and reactions. For instance, they all wanted "samples" in the form of little nubby calf horns and bits of ear leather to take home as souvenirs from the field trips. Squeamishness is something that develops, sometimes is even cultivated, at a later time. As an example, my daughter recalls that when she was four or five, my husband, his father, and Uncle Bill were butchering a beef for us. They had a tripod set up out in back where the carcass was hanging, and its head was lying in the pickup bed. Kathleen says she went out, climbed up in the pickup, and searched all over that steer's head, looking for the bullet hole! And she remembers looking at the wash tub that held the intestines and thinking, "So that's what the insides are like."

***

One last ranch trip story:

Chuck: "Hey Mom, hey Dad, guess what we did today. We went on a field trip to a cow farm. Here, read this note."

Dad: "The note says that you went on a field trip, but it doesn't mention a 'cow farm'."

Chuck: "Well, it means that we did."

Dad: "Did what?"

Chuck: "Went to a cow farm, of course. Look here!" (With that he dumped out two calf horns and a piece of ear.)

Dad: "Is this how you got spattered with blood?"

Chuck: "I guess so. Maybe I got a little too close."

Dad: "Where was this so-called 'cow farm,' and how did you get there?"

Chuck: "We went on the bus, and it was out on a dirt road."

Dad: "What did you see there?"

Chuck: "We saw cows, horses, cowboys, a fire and a hot branding iron."

Dad: "Did this serve some sort of function?"

Chuck: "I guess so that each of us kids could have them."

Dad: "Why did they brand them?"

Chuck: "So the owner knows which cows belong to him."

Dad: "Is that all you did?"

Chuck: "Well, we came home."

Chapter 24

What Did You Do Today?

Probably the answer most parents receive when they ask their child what he did at school today is: "Nothing." It was certainly the answer I usually got from my normally talkative daughter when she was in kindergarten. That response was most frustrating. Her teacher, Mrs. B., was a very experienced kindergarten teacher, and I was quite new at it. I knew that if Kathleen would tell more about her classroom activities I could find some good ideas that I could adapt into my teaching. But if I pressured her about the day's events I might get something like, "Well, Mrs. B. threw me in a mud puddle and stepped on me!"

On the other hand, I had Mrs. B.'s daughter in my class. She went home each day and gave a play-by-play report of her day. For good measure, she even threw in my Texas accent. This really didn't set well with her mom, who was from New York and seemed to think a southern accent was a sign of ignorance or inferiority, or both.

When our son, Benny, reached kindergarten, his reply if questioned was more like, "I don't remember, but I had fun!" He did volunteer that he liked the building blocks, and that there was a little girl in class "with the cutest face, but I don't remember her name."

So how does an interested parent find out about life in the kindergarten lane? Some can become volunteers and be aides for one session per week. Another possibility would be to talk with the teacher and get her point of view on the subject. But what about little Johnny's or Joanie's perspective?

Still another way is to learn to ask your child the right questions, *specific questions*. Did you hear a story? What songs did you sing? Did you play games? Make new friends? Maybe then you will get better answers than Kathleen gave her mother.

Or, you can just back off and listen. This will most likely provide you with bits and pieces of information about the things that impressed the child during the day. Then your only problem is to fit the pieces together right. One thing that Kathleen would always volunteer was, "We learned a new song today."

We find that children will generally report on the things that impress them, but not necessarily the most important things. And, since no two children are alike, each will be impressed by something different. For example, there was Mac, whose daily report to his mother was, "and after recess we had our snack, and then it was time to come home." His mother took what he said literally. There was a weight problem in that family and the children were not allowed any food between meals, which, I'm sure, was why Mac was so impressed with having snacks. But did Mom really think we could feed a child for over an hour on 25 cents per day?

This communications difficulty between parent and child prompted me to think about a solution to the problem. After all, knowing what went on in the classroom was good not only for the parents, but also for the child and the teacher. My solution? When the children were lined up to go home I would ask, "Do you know what your mom is going to ask when you get home? She is going to say, 'What did you do at school today?'"

One child, in wide-eyed wonder, asked, "How did you know that?"

"So what will you tell her? Who remembers something we

did?"

Bit by bit they would remember classroom activities, and we would piece them together. Then I would admonish them to be sure to tell Mom about it. This worked; I got positive feedback from parents from time to time. They were glad to get the child's report each day.

Earlier I referred to children being *lined up*. I found that children *like* orderliness in their lives, and they are quick to realize that there are certain times when there is a given practice to be followed, and other times when they are free to follow their own inclinations.

There are some kindergartens in which children are not given assigned seats to be occupied at "table time," but rather are allowed to roam and light wherever suits their fancy. I believe that Susie *needs* the security of knowing that, "This is my place and no one can deprive me of it. Mary wouldn't let me play with her in the housekeeping corner, but no one can move me from here—except Teacher."

A certain amount of structure helps them achieve a sense of security, and a feeling of security fosters learning. Just don't be so structured as to become rigid. Structure and freedom must be kept in balance.

Chapter 25

Zoo's Who

The trip to Reid Park Zoo in Tucson was one of our favorite kindergarten excursions. Our curriculum included a primary science/phonics/writing study about animals, so the children learned a lot in the classroom about zoo animals. Of course, seeing the animals "real" was different from the classroom studies, even different from watching them in films. So, in spite of their classroom studies, you won't believe some of the things they claim to have seen there…at least I don't, and I was with them. Skipping the usual recitation of lists of animals seen, here are some of their comments and observations.

* * *

"First, when we got to the zoo we got grouped. We saw those things with a lot of neck, what are they called. Not giraffes. Things with just sort of long necks, llamas. And we saw those big things with horns…those things the Indians killed. Yes, buffaloes!"

* * *

"The anteater was eating something that looked like dog food. Maybe it was mashed up ants."

* * *

"The 'fermingoes' only had one leg. The other leg got shot off. The ostrich shot it off!"

* * *

"...some things that go in the water. I think it was a daughter. Well, anyway, it rhymes with water." (Otter)

* * *

"One girl fell in the duck pond. I didn't really see that, so mark it out."

* * *

"Two bull elephants that had two horns on their faces."

* * *

"One funny brown chicken had hair sticking over his head and all around his legs."

* * *

"We got to see a one-hump camel. We got to hold some baby kangaroos. We saw some mountain lions and the daddy of the beasts. Oh, no, give that camel two humps. He was a two-hump camel."

* * *

"We saw laughin' akinas — is that how you call it? (hyenas) And we saw lions...'leons'...that's how you say it in Spanish."

* * *

"We saw tigers with spots. I don't know what they are called."

* * *

"Oh, boy, when I saw the otters I wished I had my goggles so I could swim under the water with them."

* * *

"Now this is silly. Greg said, 'What's your name, parrot? My name is Greg.' And the parrot said, 'Erk'!"

* * *

"I saw a crocodile and I stuck my fingers inside the gate, and he didn't even bite me, not even a little bit."

* * *

"...a bird as big as a horse with black and white feathers. It's head looked like a triangle, and had a long, long skinny neck. Yeah, an ostrich."

* * *

* * *

"There was a bingo tiger. An alligator named Fred—and he looked like a Fred."

* * *

"Saw birds with red and green heads. One bird said, 'Get away. Mom is asleep.' Saw monkeys with pink bottoms."

* * *

"I saw…what are those things with stripes? Five stripes? Never mind that. I saw a big tortoise without no teeth."

* * *

"I saw polo bears. The black panther sometimes falls off the tree to the floor—just like kids."

* * *

"The daddy lion is the one that has the wig. And a monkey sang a song for us."

* * *

"We saw wolfs that laugh. You know, 'laughing javalinas.' I saw a gorilla—if it was a gorilla. It had white all over the face. I mean on the nose and mouth and cheeks."

* * *

"We saw those big birds that have a whole bunch of wings—peacocks! And those things that look like reindeer, but they aren't…Antelopes, yeah, antelopes. And I saw one that was gray with black stripes on his tail. Wasn't a fox. Wasn't a porcupine. It was a raccoon."

* * *

"We saw a porcupine, but you could hardly see him for his pines."

* * *

"…a Pink Panther that was black."

* * *

"We saw the hippos, and they were kissing, and we saw it! And kangaroos, but just little ones, and we saw them hop." (Wallabys.)

* * *

* * *

"Saw a rhino—a two-hornded one—the wild kind!"

* * *

"The funny monkeys were saying, 'Look at the funny people out there!' And that was us!"

* * *

"Saw a calf sucking the mama cow's milk hump. Saw a lion with great big feathers around his neck."

* * *

"The elephants kept unrolling their trunks, but they would roll right back up like a yo-yo."

* * *

"The tiger should have covered his mouth when he yawned. We could see right down his throat.

"Gosh, we saw a lot. I saw horses that will bite, and one had long hair bangs. We saw rabbit-dogs. One went in a hole and had babies, and then came right back out. We saw an owl. We said 'Hi', and he said 'Hi' right back. All the animals did."

* * *

"I seen a horse with white stripes, but he had black stripes, too."

* * *

"The best part was when the rhino went to the bathroom, because they drink fifty gallons of water a day!"

* * *

"The rhinoceroses stinked, but the little rhinoceroses were cute. When the teacher blew her whistle we had to get on the bus to go home. Oh, I got one more thing to tell. Mrs. Chambers said that when we got on the freeway it was nap time, and Mommy, you weren't supposed to be talking. You were supposed to take a nap, too."

* * *

"It was a long ride to Tucson, but it was longer on the way back."

* * *

***

One last zoo report. Timmy reported, "We went to the zoo, and the panther started chasing us. The teacher came and saw the panther chasing us, and she chased the panther over the fence and back into the cage."

It's nice to be seen as heroic in the child's mind, but the zoo didn't have a panther at that time. Moreover, we teachers were all self-confessed cowards. Without a doubt, though, the child rated an A in imagination.

Chapter 26

Ma, Your Manners Are in the Mirror

Manners in our country have become much more relaxed in the last few decades, and it is our loss that this has happened. I've no objection to the relaxing of stiff formality, but that can be done without giving up good manners. After all, courtesy is the oil that keeps the machinery of social interaction running smoothly. It is a matter of helping others feel comfortable in their situation and comfortable with you. To see some of the worst examples of manners, you need only observe some of the television discussion group programs and talk shows.

I am always impressed with five-year-olds *and their parents* if the child uses "please," "thank you," "excuse me," and "I'm sorry" without prompting. It tells me that the child has parents who care enough to teach him at an early age to interact with others positively.

* * *

For those who remember the country-western song from back in the fifties, "Y'all Come"[10]—little Larry had been taught to say "please" and "thank you," but he experienced a little confusion with "you're welcome." He thought that was what the song was about. One day when another child thanked him for something, I heard him quickly reply, "Y'all come!"

* * *

I had returned to school after a few days of illness. When Shelley's mother dropped her at the school gate as usual, she came running to greet me, "Oh, Mrs. Chambers, I'm so glad to see you back in school. I do hope you're feeling better."

I was much impressed by her graciousness, and I replied, "Thank you. Yes, I'm much better."

Then, as Shelley turned to run play, she said, "My mother told me to say that."

I was still impressed, not only by the child who said it so nicely and with just the right inflection, but also by the mother who was teaching her children to be both courteous and gracious.

* * *

Ricky's mother was obviously teaching mannerliness, also, but he added his own twist to it. I had been absent one day, and on my return to school he greeted me with, "Mrs. Chambers, I'm sure glad you're here today."

"Well, thank you, Ricky. I'm glad to be back."

Then Ricky added, "Yes, I'm glad you're here, because if you weren't things would sure be in one helluva mess!"

* * *

Sometimes mother's training doesn't turn out quite as she would have hoped, even with the child's best efforts. Jason's mom had always stressed that he remember to say kind, encouraging, or uplifting things. Jason tried, but when he began second grade it was obvious that something was wrong with Mrs. T.'s face. He had known Mrs. T. on the playground last year and thought she was pretty and nice. But something was wrong now. (She was an attractive lady, but she had been stricken with Bell's palsy just before school started, which caused her face to be temporarily twisted and contorted. It gradually returned to normal over the next few weeks.)

Jason remembered his mother's admonition to always say nice things, so he said to her, "Mrs. T., I'm sure glad I'm in your class. I think you're a very nice teacher, and you're not nearly as ugly as some kids say you are!"

* * *

My daughter Kathleen, at about age eight, asked my permission to invite Jenny for lunch. I said, "That will be fine, only be sure to tell her that we're having liver and onions. If she doesn't like liver it would be better to invite her some other time." Jenny eagerly accepted the invitation, saying that liver would be fine. At lunch, she ate liver and onions with grace and gusto. But mid-afternoon when her mother came by to pick her up, Jenny ran out to the car, and as she got in I heard her say in a tone of deep disgust, "Moth-ah, guess what we had for din-nah. Liv-ah!"

Chapter 27

The Parent's Responsibility?

"That teacher is paid to teach my child. How dare she ask me to teach him to _____!" (Count to ten, read these flash cards, say his times tables, learn his address—take your pick or complete it your way.) How many times has that complaint been made? When is it justified? When is the teacher justified in making such a request or suggestion to the parents?

Having been both a parent and a teacher, and thus on both sides of the question, I take the position that whenever the teacher has adequately presented material so that most of the class has grasped or mastered it, and reasonable help has been given to those children who are having difficulty with it, then, rather than take more time from the whole class to work with one or two children, the teacher is right in requesting a little tutoring from home. "Reasonable help" is not an exact measure in that it varies with the size of the class, the number needing help, the number of aides or volunteers available to give such help, and other variables.

The other side of the coin is, would you want your child to be sitting in class just marking time, watching the clock tick off minutes, or throwing spit wads, while the teacher reteaches and re-re-teaches a lesson for the benefit of one or two children who may, or may not, be trying to learn?

The pluses on home tutoring are, first, that it helps parents keep up with the things being taught in the children's classroom. Second and more importantly, this is a way in which parents can show that they value their child's education. The lesson he learns is, "Gee, this must really be important because Mom/Dad thinks it is. They're even helping me learn it!"

My experience in making requests of this kind have been mostly very positive. In fact, I found that I frequently needed to warn parents not to pressure the child too much, and not to try to hold him to the task too long at a time; try to make it interesting, make a game out of learning.

But there always has to be an exception—the uncooperative parent.

The assignment was for the child to be able to tell where he/she lived. The parents were made aware of this expectation the day of preregistration, six months before the child would be entering school. Many children wanted to recite their addresses the first day of school, but I didn't press the issue for several weeks. As a motivation, after school pictures were taken, I would post a large street and road map of the area, and when Johnny could tell his street address, his picture would be fastened to the map at the appropriate spot. There was also the promise of a special treat when everyone had his picture on the map.

This is an easy assignment for the children who live in town. After all, something like 310 East Jones Street is not too difficult to memorize. But being a rural community, half of the children had to learn directions that might sound like "Go six miles out on Dos Cabezas Road, turn left on Sulphur Springs Road and go nine miles. Then turn right. Go half-a-mile and it's the only house there." For this assignment, a P.O. Box or a rural mailing address wouldn't do, unless the child lived in a mailbox. It really is a much more difficult assignment for a rural child, but I have had almost none who failed to learn to give directions to his home, once he was persuaded that hand motions accompanied with, "You go this way to a red barn, then that way to the third road, and then go straight up to a blue trailer," wouldn't do.

A good example of the exception was Annie, or rather Annie's mom. I had worked with Annie on the assignment at school, taking time away from 28 other children, but she really was not trying to learn it. So I sent home the note, "Please help Annie learn directions to her home." The next morning she reported, "My mom says that's too hard for me to learn."

I said, "Now, Annie, you're a smart girl. You're just as smart as these other children and they have learned theirs, and I know you can, too."

"Well, Mama says it's too hard."

So the next note asked Mom to come in for a conference. She replied that she didn't have time because she worked. But eventually I managed to catch her one day when she came to pick up Annie. She informed me that I was paid to teach her child. I explained that I had given Annie individual help on it, and that my aide had worked with her, but since Annie's address is pertinent only to Annie, it was unfair to take any more class time.

"Well, it's too hard for her."

I replied, "With your encouragement and help, I think she *can* learn it."

"Well, I still say it's too hard."

"Then evidently I have a higher opinion of her learning ability than you do," I replied.

"She doesn't have time to learn it. When we get home we have to go out and ride the horses."

"That's great. She can say the address while you're riding."

So, along with a generous sprinkling of profanity, she went through her litany of excuses: it's too long and difficult, I don't have time, I've got a job and two children, and on and on she went.

At that point I couldn't resist telling her that I understood that it took time; that a home, a job and two children was exactly what I had, but I had managed to teach mine their address anyway.

"Well, she knows the way home, so why should she have to say it?"

After several minutes of this, I lost all patience and told her, "Well, after all, she is *your* child, and it is a requirement for promotion to first grade."

Once Mama realized that learning her address was a requirement for promotion to the first grade, it wasn't too long before Annie could recite it fairly accurately.

The question might be brought up, why all the emphasis on a child being able to tell his full name, parents' names, address or directions to home, phone number, and other pertinent information? It is for the child's protection, in case he gets lost or (heaven forbid) kidnapped; or if the child becomes ill, injured, or for some reason had to be taken home by a nurse or other school personnel, a specific address is invaluable. Furthermore, a rural route and mailbox number may be okay for the mail carrier, but many ranch people live as much as two or three miles or farther from their mailboxes.

Now, back to the original question: How much teaching is the parent's responsibility? There is further discussion elsewhere about the things a child should know before starting school; but certainly any personal information (that which pertains only to that child) should be taught at home and at as early an age as possible. Also, parents should become involved in any area in which the child needs special help. Just don't attack the subject so fiercely that the child feels threatened by it. The light touch does it.

Another incident on the subject of home addresses: Jeana had quickly learned her street address before starting kindergarten and was one of the first to get her picture on the map in our classroom. Then, on a field trip to visit the police station, the policeman who talked to the children gave them a pep talk about the importance of knowing their addresses. He called on various children to tell him where they lived. But when he called on Jeana, she totally blanked out. She stumbled around trying to think of it, and finally her Sunday School training surfaced. She said, "Well, I know it *isn't* John 3:16!"[11]

Chapter 28

My Mama's Name Is Mama

As mentioned previously, kindergarten children are expected to be able to give not only their own correct names, but also their parents' names. The child's own name is seldom a problem, but they do have their own ideas about their parents' names.

* * *

Cody: "My mama is named *Mama*, and my daddy is named *Daddy*. My grandma calls my mama *Anna*, but that's not her real name. Her real name is *Mama*."

* * *

Janet couldn't think of her mother's name, so I had to fall back on an alternate method by asking, "What does your daddy call your mother?" She answered, "My daddy calls my mama *Woman*—like, '*Woman*, come here.'"

* * *

I was trying to get Mary to remember her parent's last name. She finally informed me, "She's only got two names. One is *Eleanor*, and the other is *Mama*. That's all the names she's got!"

* * *

Carolyn seemed to think that her father had only a last name. I asked, "Well, Carolyn, what does your mother call your father when she wants to tell him something?"

She answered, "*Anderson*, I mean it!"

* * *

Danny: "My mom's name is *Honey*. I know, 'cause that's what Daddy calls her."

* * *

"I don't know why y'all keeps a-sayin' that us Jones kids ain't got no daddy. We do too have a daddy, and his name is *Mr. Brown*."

* * *

And Carl insisted that his father's first name was *Mister*.

Chapter 29

Ghost Feathers and Cow Stuff

Children have their own ideas about sickness and health, doctors and nurses, safety, cleanliness, and shots. Especially shots. Every year the health department nurses came to school to give booster shots to those who needed them. Can you imagine taking 20 five-year-olds to get shots, all at the same time? What happens if one bursts into tears or throws a tantrum? Do the others all join in?

Actually, most children are very brave about getting their shots and few of my students ever cried. The secret? A wonderful pep talk before we left the classroom, assuring them that it helped if they looked away, but it was all right to say "ouchie." And suckers were promised for everyone who did not cry. (One sucker a year is not going to ruin their teeth.)

I hugged each child as he or she got the shot, turning their heads so they could not watch, and praising them for being so brave. The suckers helped, too. In all my years of teaching kindergarten and first grade, only two or three times did I have a child cry. I do remember one who got so hysterical on the way to the nurse's room that the nurse didn't even attempt the shot. I have always wondered about the history which led to that performance.

One child's comment: "I got a shot right in the blood!"

***

A few days after the children had been given T.B. skin tests:

School Nurse: "Children, I've come to read your arms today, so get ready to show me your arm where you got the shot."
Aaron (after the nurse checked his arm): "I don't think she read my arm 'cause no one had written on it."
Marc: "Well, I don't want my arm red—I want mine green!"
Marc was also the one who didn't want his eyes checked. He liked his brown.

***

When my own son Benny was enduring the labors of learning to read and write in the first grade he announced to me, "When I'm grown I'm going to be a scientist. And I'm going to invent a vaccine to give the mothers a shot before her baby is born. Then the baby will be born knowing all this stuff and won't have to go to school." I asked, "Wouldn't it be better to wait and give the baby the shot?" "Nope," he said, "Babies don't like shots. The mom should have it."

***

Debbie: "My voice is sore today."

***

We were somewhat puzzled, but also amused, when a little Navajo girl, after being ill a few days, reported that the medicine man had given her "mud" to drink, and tickled her stomach with "ghost feathers."

I don't know what those were, but does it sound any stranger than this from a child whose parents had a well-educated Anglo background? Said he, "Our wetback (meaning their farm laborer from Mexico) stepped on a nail, but it's okay 'cause my Mom put some of that soft cow stuff on it."

***

The children loved the school nurse and liked an excuse to visit with her in her office.

Karen: "Mrs. Chambers, quick! May I go to the nurse before

this scratch gets infected?"

* * *

Darrin: "I need to go see the nurse. My brain hurts."

* * *

Greg: "Teacher, I need to go let the nurse measure me again. I grew some more last night."

* * *

On the subject of dentists:

Lisa: "I'm going to the dentist to get some cavities put in."

Carolyn: "I went to the dentist to get my tooth stuffed."

Kenny: "My daddy is going to the dentist to get his tonsils out."

Rodney: "I had to go to the dentist because my sister hit me in the seat and bent my tooth."

* * *

At Halloween we were discussing Halloween costumes and safety. The children made some suggestions:

Kim: "Be sure to wear something white so you can be seen."

Maria: "Don't wear something that will make you trip and fall."

Sue: "Carry a flashlight, not a candle."

Chuck: "I know another dangerous thing about Halloween costumes. Zippers. Zippers are dangerous because you might get your penis caught in it, and that hurts. It happened to me once!"

* * *

Sylvia: "It's better to be fat than skinny. Fat people are more healthier and live longer. And if you've got a fat head you can think better!"

* * *

When little Joe came back from the restroom without stopping at the sink to wash his hands, I reminded him to do so. He said, "But, Teacher, I don't need to wash my hands. I didn't pee on them."

* * *

Roy: "Hey, Teacher, I had the neatest Christmas vacation. And do you know why? I didn't have to take a single bath the whole two weeks!"

* * *

In a discussion about milk it was mentioned that milk doesn't have to come from a cow; some people use milk from other animals. The children remembered some of our social studies films— that Eskimos use reindeer milk, and people in the Mideast deserts use camel milk. It was also mentioned that some people with allergies find that goat's milk helps them.

Then little Mary informed us, "Rabbits' milk is pretty good, too. I never drank any, but I know it grows good rabbits!"

* * *

When we talked about eating a good breakfast Jeff informed us, "That's not the way cowboys do it. They just go down to the river and wash their faces, and they drink some whiskey for breakfast."

* * *

Everything was going smoothly in Mrs. T's second grade when suddenly little Kevin burst into tears. Mrs. T. rushed to his side to see what the problem was. Putting her arms around him, she asked all the usual questions. Did he feel sick, did his head hurt? Did another child take something of his? To each question he sobbed out, "No."

"Well, can you tell me what *is* wrong?" she asked. Finally, between sobs, he managed to tell Mrs. T., "I forgot to take my courage pill this morning."

* * *

How about a little medical fiction from kindergarten?

Kendra: "You know, my friend had a heart attack, and when they took him to the hospital the doctors fixed his heart back with toothpicks. But the toothpicks slipped out, and he died!"

Chapter 30

The Big D — Discipline

The word *discipline* is often thought of as meaning punishment. However, its primary meaning is *teaching; training that corrects, molds, or perfects mental or moral character.* Punishment is a secondary meaning of the word.

Discipline at Home

We've all chuckled over the Abbott and Costello dialogue about baseball, with the confusion of "Who" being the name of the first baseman. But when the problem is not "Who's on first," but rather, "Who is in charge?", whether at home or at school, confusion reigns and big trouble is ahead.

Many adults have created chaos and havoc in their own lives and in the lives of children by failing to discern that with children true democracy cannot succeed. The child will vote for instant gratification every time. To expect a child to be able to postpone the pleasure of the moment for the sake of some distant benefit is unrealistic.

What preschool child has the understanding, much less the inner strength of self-discipline to pass up a candy bar because it might contribute to a tooth cavity at some indefinite time in the future? Or, when TV is so alluring at 8:00 or 9:00 p.m., can a child project himself into the fatigue of tomorrow morning?

He can't. Therefore, "Who" had better be on first, meaning the adult must be the one to take the responsibility for guiding decisions until the child gains the maturity and wisdom to make good decisions for himself.

The child should be given opportunities to make choices *within limits*, beginning gradually while he is small. For instance, the choice is not whether or not to get dressed, but rather whether to wear the red shirt or the blue one. And very importantly, once the child has made a decision, he must abide by it.

If the child decides that he doesn't like what Mom serves for lunch and therefore won't eat it, he has made a decision. Whether he sits there while the rest of the family eats, or is excused from the table, should be according to your family rules. But he should never be given a substitute food unless Mom wants to become a short-order cook for the rest of her life. Nor should he be allowed to eat anything until the next regular eating time. Don't worry, missing one meal won't cause malnutrition. Yes, he'll complain that he's hungry, but the answer should be, "But it was *your* choice not to eat lunch, so no food until dinner." No nagging—just a statement of fact.

If the parent gives in when the child whines, complains, threatens, or throws tantrums, then you'll know that the child is the one in charge. That's not fair. That's giving the child more responsibility than he can handle, and at the same time lessening his ability to become a responsible adult.

We constantly hear about the increase in child abuse. Sometimes we meet it face to face when a child comes to school with suspicious looking injuries, and we are horrified and repulsed. The experts tell us that in most cases the parents don't intend to beat up on their child, they just lose control. I believe this problem has two major underlying causes. First, undisciplined children grow up to become undisciplined adults and parents. Second, undisciplined adults cannot possibly raise children to have self-discipline. It is a vicious circle, because it takes a mountain of parental self-discipline to be reasonable, fair, considerate, and especially consistent. Many times, because of time pressures, fatigue, or immediate circumstances, it *seems* easier to let an infraction slide. But, the parents will pay later if they fail to be consistent in their discipline. A good parent must always be the "Who" that is on first.

But being in charge has its limits and does not mean oppressive dictatorship. I remember an extreme case that still staggers my imagination. A handsome, normally intelligent kid I will call Hector, entered my class at mid-year. A few days as an onlooker in a new situation is not unusual, but Hector continued to sit like a bump on a log day after day unless I specifically called him by name, "Hector, come join us here on the rug for a story." Or, "Hector, come now, it's singing time." If it was a worksheet assignment, he could see all the others go right to work, but he would never pick up his pencil until I said, "Hector, do you understand what you are to do?...Then get busy." Even on the playground he had to be prompted into any activity, even to try the slide or monkey bars.

I asked his parents to come in for a conference, but only the father came. Looking back, I suspect that the mother wasn't allowed to come. His explanation of the child's behavior? "Sure, I have taught him not to ever do anything until *I* say that he can. I'm a guard at Fort Grant Prison and I see all those fellows that are in trouble because their parents let them do things without permission. So I've taught Hector not to ever do *anything* without my permission!"

Since Hector was physically well and within the average range mentally, I would guess that this kind of compliance was achieved only by psychological and emotional abuse which was probably preceded by physical abuse.

I talked with the school counselor about this conference, but the family moved shortly thereafter. What happened to Hector? Did he become a pliable, non-resistant, mindless blob of nothing? Or when he reached his teens and became a match for his father in size, did he rebel? One wonders.

So parents must remember—for the child, allow choices within limits; for themselves, set limits on their limiting. Balance is the key. Remember "Who's" on first.

Discipline in the Classroom

Ideally, kindergarten would be a happy place at all times where all would be kindness and love, cooperation and progress, and correction would never be necessary. But like everything else, the ideal is never quite achieved. I always tried to establish the guidelines for acceptable behavior at the beginning of the year and maintain them with positive feedback. However, there are always times....

In the classroom, a child who starts getting out of hand can usually be brought back just by making eye contact with him for a moment. Or if the children are working at their tables and one begins to feel mischievous, just to pass by and touch him on the shoulder or give him a little pat on the head usually will suffice. Or speaking the child's name may do the trick; insert it in the middle of a sentence if you are talking to the group, or even if you are reading a story. It should bring Johnny back in line every time.

If these tricks are insufficient, isolating an offender is usually quite effective. The popular term for that is "time-out." Many teachers just use a special chair away from the class. I always found it to be most effective if the offender was *in* the classroom, but *out of sight* of the other children. In one classroom where I taught I had my piano angled across a corner of the room. Behind the piano made a good place for a child to think over behavior problems. One day the principal dropped in with a message for his granddaughter while she was "serving time" behind the piano. He knew her well, and he approved.

Another time, when a child needed a little time-out, I designated the space under my desk as the "baby box." (Teachers never have a chance to sit during the teaching day anyway.) My rationale, which I explained to the children, was that kindergartners are no longer babies; they are big boys and girls, big enough to go to school. Babies don't know how to control their hands or their mouths; but children who are old enough for school can. But if someone got "little" again and couldn't control his mouth or his hands or feet, then he was acting like a baby, and the "baby box" was the place for him.

I found this more effective than an isolation chair because he could hear the lesson, his attention could not be visually distracted (nothing very interesting about the space under the desk), and he *could not* distract the attention of the other children. Five minutes' time-out in the "baby box" usually gave the child enough time to regain self-control.

One lesson I learned about disciplining children was not to ask or expect a Mexican or Native American child to look at me while being reprimanded. This is a cultural difference that is ingrained in the child before he reaches school age.

As a child, I was taught that whenever my parents talked to me, especially if I was being corrected, I was to give them my full attention, signified by looking them in the eye. Not to do so indicated that I was looking for a way out rather than listening. Likewise, when my children were growing up, I expected eye contact from them whenever serious conversation was the order of the day. And at school, if an Anglo child was on the receiving end of some "straight talk," eye contact from the child was automatic, unless he was tuning you out. Then I would say, "Look at me when I'm talking to you." And eye contact would be reestablished.

But with a Mexican or Native American child—no way! Start scolding and he would look down; he absolutely would not look at me. Even when I said, "Look at me," it was as though he simply could not. Then I learned that in certain cultures, for a child to look at you when being reprimanded was considered impudence. (However, this did not apply to those whose families had been in our area for two or three generations; they had adapted themselves to the Anglo ways.)

Was I practicing racism by expecting eye contact from Anglos but not from Mexicans or Native Americans? I think not. This was a cultural difference that I learned to respect.

I administered a few spankings—back in the days when teachers were allowed to use discretion and common sense in managing their classrooms. I will say only this about spankings or any other disciplinary practices: the more they are used the less effective they become. However, when a child is deliberately misbehaving, or if the child is clearly out of control, there is nothing that settles the matter and clears the air as effectively as a quickly administered spanking, on the spot, so that the child sees (and feels) the connection between his misdeed and the sting of pain.

But notice, I didn't say *beating*; I said *spanking*. There is a difference; spanking gives momentary pain, beating inflicts bodily harm. And yes, there has to be a reasonable amount of pain. If there is no pain, you might as well give him a pat on the back and say, "Okay, go ahead. Nobody really cares about how you act."

The quick pain of a spanking that settles the matter and clears the air is much less destructive than a nagging lecture that goes on and on. A spanking administered to a small child in the principal's office after two days of red tape is useless at best. There are other ways to teach a child self-control; and self-control (self-discipline) must begin with external discipline. Whatever method is used, it must be sufficiently unpleasant that the child will strive to avoid it. And there must be no doubt that the penalty is *certain* if he misbehaves.

* * *

One spanking that I remember giving involved Jan, a beautiful little blonde who considered first grade a wonderful social encounter. And she was sociable. On this particular day her number one social partner was absent, so while she should have been doing her seat work, it was chatter, chatter, chatter with Julie, and neither one was getting the assignment done. Julie was normally a rather quiet child, very eager to please, and she really didn't know how to handle Jan's constant attention and chatter.

I was trying to conduct a reading class with another group of students. After reminding Jan for the umpteenth time to quit talking and get busy, I promised her, "Disrupt this class one more time and I *will* spank you." And sure enough, I had to carry through.

"Jan, you come here." And both girls came. I turned Jan over my lap and paddled her with my hand. I didn't intend to spank Julie; it was Jan who was doing the talking. But as soon as I let Jan up, Julie threw herself over my lap for her spanking, too. What should I do? Well, I gave her a little half-hearted spanking. Then, crying, she threw her arms around my neck and told me she loved me. And we both cried!

* * *

And then there was Carla, a bright and charming girl, really a nice child, but not perfect, contrary to mother's opinion. Along in mid-winter, Carla was ill and missed several weeks of school. When she returned, Carla thought she was a princess and above obeying class rules. I knew a spanking was inevitable but postponed it as long as possible because I felt it would precipitate a confrontation with the mother. Eventually it could be postponed no longer, so I spanked her. Then her attitude was, "Okay, now that I've had my spanking, I can do as I please." And she really got obnoxious. I knew that I had to show her that one spanking doesn't give immunity.

So Carla got another spanking, making two in one day. That settled her down. In fact, she was a well-behaved child the rest of the year. (And no confrontation with the mother followed. I later asked the mother if Carla had told about getting two spankings in one day. She hadn't, she was too smart for that. And meanwhile, Mom had caught on that her daughter wasn't perfect.)

* * *

We had taken the class to the activity room to show films. After a few minutes Kelly said she had to go to the restroom, which meant going back to the classroom. When she had not returned after several minutes I told Mrs. E. to stay with the class, and I went to check on Kelly. When I got to the room, I found Kelly doing a little "investigative work"—investigating the contents of my purse. What do you do in a case like this? She hadn't taken anything yet, and I didn't know her intentions. I wasn't quite sure how to handle this, so I said, "Kelly, why are you into my purse? Do you think there is something of yours in there? Let's see. Is this your handkerchief? Is this comb yours? Is this your wallet? Is this your allergy medicine?"

I showed her the entire contents of my purse, and of course, her answer was no to every question, even to the little handful of change in my wallet. (I was glad that was all I was carrying that day.) Then I told her she must never, ever even look in my desk again for anything; if she thought that something of hers was there to come tell me about it. And that settled the matter.

* * *

Whenever two children had a matter they couldn't settle, it usually worked just to have them stand facing each other, with fingertips on each other's shoulders and with instructions *not* to smile at each other. In less than a minute they would both be laughing and ready to be friends again.

Occasionally there would be a case where this didn't work, and so it was with Ricky and Pedro. They were always at odds. I got tired of settling their disputes, so one day I looked at the two boys. They were pretty well matched for size. I said, "Okay, you two are determined to fight, so come up here and fight." But right away I had to stop them.

Yes, they were the same size, but I had failed to take into account that Ricky was the youngest in the class, barely five. Although he was exceptionally bright, already reading, his coordination in general was very immature. In fact, he walked and ran like a *young* four-year-old. Pedro, on the other hand, was nearly six, and although small, he was extremely well coordinated and knew how to use his fists. We settled their problem another way.

The moral of the story is: Be sure to consider all the factors involved. That's always a good thing to do.

* * *

Mack loved to spit on people. He had been reprimanded on the playground for this several times, even sent to stand alone by the fence, but still he persisted. Then one day he spit on another child in the classroom. I called him back to one corner, handed him a paper cup, and told him, "Mack, you really do seem to have a lot of spit, more than you know what to do with. So you just stand right here and spit in this paper cup. Spit until you have a whole cupful."

And the rest of the class went ahead with the lessons while Mack worked at his spitting for about an hour. Of course, he never came near filling the cup, but that took care of the excess saliva for the rest of the year.

* * *

For safety reasons it was imperative that children not run on the patio; the biggest danger was that they would frequently crash into the large metal poles that supported the patio roof. We tried hard to enforce that rule, but it is as natural for children to run as it is to breathe.

One day I had sent several rule-breakers back to the classroom door with instructions to *walk* to the playground. Jenny had to be sent back twice to walk, not run, on the patio. As she passed me on her way to the playground I heard her muttering to herself, "Just a-wearin' out my shoes! Just a-wearin' out my shoes!"

* * *

But my favorite way to handle a problem was the way I handled Donnie's. He was a child with mixed-up feelings; mixed up about himself and the whole world. His parents were divorced and remarried. He couldn't live with Mom because stepfather didn't want him, but his sisters were okay. So he lived with his dad, stepmom (who accepted him only as part of a package deal), and two stepsisters. Even with Grandma he rated rather low, way below his sisters. A real, live, five-year-old persona non grata. Consequently, he seemed to think that people, especially Teacher, should be constantly reminded of his presence. In other words, a disruptive child.

It took me several days and a few prayers to figure out how to help him feel better about himself. My solution was this: whenever he began disruptive behavior, in the middle of whatever we were doing, I would turn to him and ask, "Donnie, have you had a hug today?" The answer was always no, so I would say, "Well, come here. I have a hug for you." The hug would calm him down for a while, and when he began to be disruptive again, the process was repeated. At first he required perhaps 8 or 10 hugs a day, but it gradually tapered off to one or two a day, and finally one or two hugs a week. (And we all need at least that many.)

Of course, a lot of other children would line up for hugs, too. But that was all right. I had hugs for all who wanted them, and the results were worth the time it required. It was great to watch Donnie gain a feeling of self-worth and to develop self-control. Can you think of a more gratifying way to discipline?

* * *

To sum up the matter of discipline, one must first consider the child's intentions. Did he accidentally spill the glass of milk, or did he dump it on purpose? Most of a small child's misdeeds occur from immature coordination, immature judgment or immature self-control, not from deciding deliberately, "I'm going to do something bad."

Punishment won't cure immaturity; punishment should be reserved for deliberate misdeeds or defiance. Then it is time to show the child who is in control. And remember, the parents of a small child have the God-given responsibility to be in control. And for a teacher, it's part of the job description.

* * *

It is best to try to foresee where problems might arise and avoid them when it is practical to do so. There are enough unavoidable situations to deal with, so eliminate the trivial.

When reasonable to do so, allow *natural consequences* to teach the lesson. When natural consequences are too severe (you wouldn't deliberately allow a child to stick his fingers into a fan, for example), then try to find a logical consequence. (No cool air from the fan for you, kid!) In other words, try to make the punishment fit the crime. And when that doesn't seem feasible, perhaps you can be creative in your discipline. I remember a bit of "creative discipline" from my childhood. My sister and I had committed some transgression. Our dad had us move the woodpile from one side of the yard to the other, which took our after-school playtime for two or three evenings. Then he said, "Now, move it back again!"

With all discipline, and especially if it is a spanking, be sure that *training* the child is the intent. When it becomes a means for the adult to vent his frustration, that's when there is, not a possibility, but a *probability* of child abuse occurring.

* * *

We would all prefer not to have to administer punishment, but, to quote Edward A. Wynne, Professor of Education, University of Illinois at Chicago, "Without effective punishment, childish misconduct cannot be prohibited; only the real threat of punishment gives prohibition meaning. The characteristics of effective punishments are simple: They must be unpleasant, easy to administer, capable of being carried out immediately after the offense, susceptible to being given in doses of increasing intensity and not notably cruel."

For effective discipline, first be sure the rules are reasonable, fair, and consistent with the child's developmental level. Second, be sure the child knows the rules and understands the "whys." Third, be consistent, consistent, consistent. And above all, let the child know you *love* him, love him enough to help him become the best person he can be.

* * *

The best book on this subject, one I highly recommend, is *Dare to Discipline*[12], by James Dobson, Ph.D., published by Tyndale House Publishers, Wheaton, Illinois. Or the very newly published *The New Dare to Discipline*[13], by the same author. Available in paperback. (Also in hardcover — in case you still feel that you need a paddle!)

Chapter 31

Mary, Mary, Quite Contrary

What does your garden grow? According to the kindergarten rumors there are things growing there that would certainly surprise the owners. We learned from their field trip reports that, in addition to the usual, garden-variety tomatoes, beans, okra, corn, et cetera, they saw:

- dilly peppers and honey berries
- green pomatoes and butatoes
- megatation
- okree
- lettuce that grows underground
- stuff that's bumpy and kinda yellow, but it turns green
- a hot sauce plant
- a blueberry tree
- green long-pointy vegetables
- something with a little green on top and some yellow on bottom
- bikini squash
- eggplants…eggs grow in eggplants
- corn on a bean stalk
- a pumpkin tree
- a corn tree
- some mari-flowers
- squash soup…that's something you can grow
- spaghetti watermelon
- bermatoes and pumprams
- chili bells

* * *

"Do you think we go by fields for a field trip? No, we don't. We go by gardens. Do you know my partner? I don't either. What are those things called that are kinda like a ball with a string on the bottom? They're not really balls. Tulips? No, turnips! What are you writing down, Mom? You're not supposed to write while I'm talking to you. It's not manners."

* * *

"Saw some flowers called Mary-orange. You know, it vibrates the bugs and kills 'em!" (Marigolds are said to discourage insects in the garden.)

* * *

"We saw pumpkins. It's really called a jack-o-lantern when it has a face."

* * *

"Black-eyed peas... they look at you."

* * *

"The cucumbers are pickles 'til you cook 'em."

* * *

"There were bees too, but they didn't bite me. Bumblebees."

* * *

"We saw two old ladies. They were our teachers."

* * *

"I didn't see nothing. There wasn't nothing there. The peaches smelled terrible. We were gone nine hours. I enjoyed the trip."

* * *

"Some of that stuff you make popcorn with, 'cept it was all rusty."

* * *

"I saw butatoes, you know, them brown things...*butatoes*. And peaches and limes. What are limes? Seen a cherry vine. Ain't that neat! Onions. And them little tiny balls that have seeds in them, and you swallow the seeds. The cover on them is red, and all that juice comes out, and it's good. What are they? *Tomatoes*? That's it, tomatoes."

* * *

"Inside the green beans are seeds. You eat them. The peaches have one seed. The apples have lots of seeds — black seeds that look like an eye. Watermelons has black seeds. Pumpkins have yellow seeds. Tomatoes you eat with the seeds. And the pear has a little bone which you can't see. The pear has a tail that you're not supposed to eat. The carrot just has vitamins — no seeds."

* * *

"He grows cheese. I mean he makes cheese from corn. He cuts a hole in the corn and puts cheese in it. Then he puts the top on it and cooks it in the oven. He puts salt and pepper on it and eats it."

In order to visit one garden we had to go through the owner's patio, and on the patio hung a cage with a—well— here are the descriptions:

"They had a pet parrot, or some kind of bird. It was white."

"I saw a pigeon that they caught."

"You know what? The little boy that lives there has a bird-chicken, or chicken-bird, or something like that. It's white."

"We saw a ca-ca-roo-di-du."

"They had an animal in a cage."

(Actually, this creature was a white pigeon. At least they agreed on the color!)

* * *

"It was a hot trip, at least a hundred and eighty degrees."

* * *

"It was lots of fun, and it's a heck of a lot better garden than yours, Mom!"

Chapter 32
Kindergarten Stew

No, not stewed kindergartners, but stew made *by* kindergartners. This always followed a study about our nutritional needs and food sources, including a visit to a garden and to the produce section of a local market. There we looked at the vegetables, helping the children become more aware of some vegetables which perhaps were not used in their own homes. Also, we would purchase the vegetables and meat needed to make our famous stew the next day.

As you will surmise, most children were more impressed by a look behind the scenes in the meat department than by the vegetables.

* * *

"We went to Rey's Market, and a lady who works there said, 'What do we have here?' And then one of us said, 'It's a gang of kindergarten class.' A grocer is a man who works in the grocery store. Stores are for people to buy stuff like food and milk so you can eat. The thing they check you out with is a register."

"Saw some carrots, but no marshmallows. We even went back to where it was cold, and the heaters were going, and that's what made it cold."

"We didn't went on a field trip. We saw some lechuga (lettuce). Then I saw some blue watermelons! Do you know blue watermelons? You know feet from cows? They killed them, and they hang them on a hook by the feet—they hook them."

* * *

"We got to go in the meat thingamabobby."

* * *

"I learned how to make hamburger. Put meat in a machine and it comes out like spaghetti. When we made our stew at school we cut the vegetables with scissors. That's more safer."

* * *

"Let me tell you how big them things are. The back legs of the cow goes from the floor all the way to the tiptop roof. We bought some stuff, some meat. Oh, I remember, it was a pork chop."

"It was cold, cold, cold in there... I think 55 milligrams in the meat."

* * *

"We went to a pig. It was hanging by the feet. It had a nose and mouth."

* * *

"We learned that tomatoes are a fruit *and* a vegetable. I'm not going to school tomorrow because they have things that I don't like in the stew, like cabbage." (Note: she was there, helped make stew, and ate it with gusto.)

* * *

"The man showed us cherry tomatoes and he said they were marbles. Man, was he ever funny! Saw some broccoli that looked like a tree."

* * *

"Them yellow things weren't peaches. Just write, 'I don't know what them yellow things were."

"Write whatever Jenny (his twin) said; we saw the same things."

* * *

"We saw big, big elephant feet—or pieces of meat, really big, really huge!"

* * *

"We got some bologna for our soup. We're going to have chocolate milk with it.

"And we learned about being nice. We saw *hot* peppers and *chilly* peppers."

* * *

"Are bananas vegetables? We went by the charger but I didn't get to buy anything. I got an orange sucker, but I like red! Me and my friend were the bringer-uppers 'cause we're always way, way late at the line. Sometimes we have to walk with girls, but don't write that down or I'll be mad at you!"

* * *

"What did we learn on this trip? Well, we learned not to walk in the street, and not to push, and to watch out for cars, and to be nice."

* * *

"We bought some vegetables to make Rock Stew. We had more fun than going to the store with you, Mommy!"

Chapter 33

Little Round Green Things

The last several years that I taught, we moved beyond the usual kindergarten milk-and-crackers snack to a nutrition program that provided for a wide variety of foods in place of the graham cracker or cookie. This program met a real need because our school district was very large with at least half the children being bused in from farms and ranches, some riding as far as fifty miles each way. This meant a very early breakfast and a very late lunch. Or, for afternoon class children, a very early lunch and a long time until dinner. Kindergartners have small tummies and high metabolism rates. Children don't learn well on empty tummies; they do need a little snack between meals.

We planned these snacks to be nutritionally sound, generally avoiding sweets. We used the opportunity to introduce new foods, especially vegetables, to the children. We found that they overcame a lot of food prejudices and learned to try new foods. There was only one rule: "You must take three bites of the food." I explained to them that if it was a new food they probably would not think they liked the first bite because food never tastes the way it looks.

The second bite would not seem so strange, and the third bite would be the one that would tell them if they liked the food or not. If they still didn't like it, they didn't have to eat any more, but there were usually seconds for those who wanted more. Actually the "three bites" rule was not enforceable; we would never think of trying to force a child to eat. But it worked quite well, and my aide was exceptionally good at coaxing a reluctant child to try the food. However, coaxing was seldom needed.

* * *

At our Mother's Day tea in May, instead of cookies, we served punch and finger foods, such as cauliflower, carrot sticks, and "ants on a log" which are celery sticks filled with peanut butter with a few raisins on top. It was interesting and amusing to watch children as they accompanied their mothers along the refreshment table. Obviously, some who had learned to thoroughly enjoy veggies at school had kept it a deep, dark secret from Mom.

They would glance up at Mom, look at the veggies, just almost drooling, look back at Mom, and again at the food. You could almost see the wheels turning as they pondered. "Shall I take some and let Mom find out that I like this, or shall I pass it by like I do at home and just go hungry?" Most would reveal their secret; a few would opt for hunger.

* * *

We tried, as much as possible, to tie the snacks in with our instructional program. For example, if we were introducing the letter *B*, our snack might be bananas. This helped the child learn to associate the letter with its sound, a good beginning for phonics.

Sometimes our snack coordinated with our social studies. Near the beginning of school we would visit a garden, and for several days our snack would be various vegetables. Then would follow the wonderful "Kindergarten Stew" which the children helped prepare. This was always a big event, and I never saw a child who didn't like it.

As Thanksgiving approached we would have "Native American foods," hominy, clam chowder, jerky, and of course, turkey and cranberries.

Some children don't know their colors when starting school, so as we learned the various colors, we had foods to match. We even applied math skills to our snacks. The helpers (children whose turn it was to set tables, set out the milk, et cetera) improved their counting skills as they placed five pieces of that day's offering at each child's place.

Or, take two children, a cupcake, and a knife. One cuts the cupcake in *half* and the other chooses which half he wants. Can the "cutter" get the two halves equal? You'd better believe it! However, I once saw a child very deliberately cut way off center. I said nothing, but I wondered, did she just not care for chocolate cupcake; or had she been taught to not take the largest piece, and thus, assumed that her partner would take the small piece leaving the large piece for her? He didn't.

* * *

One thing we had to watch for was the allergy factor. Parents were asked to provide us with a list if their child had food allergies so we could give him a substitute if that food was being served. We found that most children were very good to remind us, if necessary, when the snack was one of their allergies. Very few would try to cheat on that, although some children who had no allergies would cry, "Allergy!" if they thought they weren't going to like the food.

* * *

From time to time we had interesting little side dramas concerning the snacks. I remember:

I sat at my desk doing a little paperwork as the children chatted sociably while having their mid-morning snack, which happened to be little cracker-and-*deviled-ham* sandwiches. Suddenly I realized that a deathly silence had fallen upon the table nearest me. I looked up to see that the children had all laid down their sandwiches and turned a rather sickly-looking green. That is, all except Terry who was staunchly and firmly declaring, "It is. I know it is. My mom told me what this stuff is. It's called *devil's hand*!"

* * *

We were studying the letter *O*. We had oranges one day, and the next, to introduce a different vegetable, we had fried okra. As usual, we gave very small servings, with seconds for those who wished.

Jean was a cute, smart, and badly spoiled child, the youngest of five. Her mother had told me that at home she cooked for the family according to what Jean liked. (Imagine leaving the nutritional needs of the family up to the whims of a five-year-old!) Well, Jean balked at the fried okra, and even my aide, who was ever-so-skilled at persuading reluctant children to try just one teeny little bite, couldn't get Jean to try it. Okay, so you drop it at that.

But, the next day Jean came with a note which she had wheedled her mom into writing. Jean didn't remember the name of the vegetable, but she had described it. Mom had written (tongue in cheek), "Jean is not to eat any of the little round green things."

When I read the note, I knew Jean had outsmarted herself this time, and I promptly changed the snack plans. I sent my aide to purchase Thompson's seedless green grapes for that day. Of course, none were put at Jean's place, only her milk. When she complained, "I didn't get any snack," the answer was, "But Jean, your mom said you were not to eat little round green things!"

I heard her mutter, "But I didn't mean grapes." (Some rounds the teacher wins!)

* * *

Frequently the child's ethnic background showed up in his food concepts:

Teacher:" Shall we use forks or spoons to eat our beans?"
Debbie: "I think a fork."

Joshua: "I think a spoon."
Pedro: "I'd rather eat it with a tortilla!"

* * *

Janelle was a child who was expert at saying the wrong thing. In fact, I learned to always listen whenever she opened her mouth because you never knew what was going to come out. At our Christmas party our room mother, whose husband happened to be a school board member, served apple cider with the refreshments.

Janelle: "Oh, I know what this is. It's sour beer. My daddy drinks sour beer all the time, and he gets so-o-o drunk!"

Teacher: "No, Janelle. This is not sour beer. It's apple juice, and it is perfectly all right to drink."

Janelle (after taking a sip): "Hey, this is good. It won't make little girls drunk, just boys and men."

Teacher: "Janelle, this is apple juice. It is *not* beer. It is apple juice, and it will not make you drunk. It is good for you."

Janelle (after draining her cup): "That's good. I want some more. I don't care if it does make me drunk."

Teacher to horrified room mother: "Wait until this story circulates around town. Won't it make good gossip!"

Room mother (with a shudder): "What will you say when you're asked about it?"

Teacher: "Oh, I'll just tell them that my room mother served it, and she's a school board member's wife!"

* * *

It was a Friday morning, and our snack budget for the week was pretty well depleted. We hadn't specifically planned what we would serve that day, assuming we would work out something with supplies on hand. Mrs. D. said, "Well, let's see what we have here." We found that we had white bread and some cream cheese, so obviously it would be cream cheese on white bread. Tasty, but not very interesting. Then I discovered 'way in the back of the refrigerator, a package of shredded coconut.

"Hey, this is perfect! We're studying *S* this week. We can trim off the crusts so the sandwiches are all white, then sprinkle them with coconut. And there you are, a good *S* snack, Snow-Storm Sandwiches!" I said.

We were feeling pretty smug about the wonderful *S* snack we had just concocted until we heard little Tommy say, "Well, look what they're feeding us today, *sponges!*"

(Well, *sponge* is an *S* word, too!)

* * *

When we were studying the letter *V*, a mother whose husband was an avid hunter brought a venison roast from her freezer for the snack. In the discussion of venison the teacher realized that the children didn't understand that venison is deer meat. She said, "Sometimes the name of meat is not the same as the animal it comes from. For instance, meat from cattle is called beef, and meat from pigs is called pork. Meat from sheep is called mutton, but who knows what animal venison comes from?"

No one knew.

"I'll give you a hint," said the teacher. "It's what your mother sometimes calls your father."

"Don't eat it!" screamed one child. "It's jackass!"

Chapter 34

I Wasn't Eavesdropping

But What I Heard Was Sometimes Interesting, Amusing or Even Enlightening

James was trying to impress Mary. "So I took my bean shooter and went out hunting. And I saw this bird, so I loaded my bean shooter and aimed at that bird. And he just folded his wings and said his prayers, and fell over dead!"

* * *

Frank: "Me and my brother built a snowman."

Norma (correcting Frank's grammar): "Frank, it's 'My brother and *I*...'"

Frank: "Why, Norma, I didn't know you had a brother!"

* * *

Hank: "I'm going to marry Betty, and Michelle, too."
Bill: "But you can't marry two people."
Hank: "Yes, I'm going to marry both of them."
Bill: "But my mom says they'll put you in jail."
Hank: "Then I'll marry them both, but we'll let Michelle be the sister."

* * *

At free-play time some children were staging a spontaneous wedding. They were all dressed for the occasion in dress-up clothing from the collection in the housekeeping center. I heard the bride-to-be say to the prospective groom, "Get that dumb belt from around your neck if you want to marry me! Here, put on this necktie."

Then the groom said to the preacher, "Well, you've got to wear a tie, too, if you're going to perform this wedding!"

Then, when they all felt they were appropriately attired I heard the preacher ask the groom, "Do you take this lovely wedding girl to be your *awful* wedded wife?"

* * *

Arthur announced, "I've been in kindergarten two weeks, and I haven't got a single one of those girls pregnant yet!"

(Makes you wonder about the conversation at home, doesn't it?)

* * *

Someone had used some undesirable language and the children were discussing "dirty language" and "dirty minds." Sylvia announced, "I don't have a dirty mind. Mine is clean. I wash it with detergent and scrub it with Clorox!"

* * *

The children were discussing what they wanted to be when they grew up:

Andrea: "When I grow up I want to be a store helper."
Dale: "That's so you could eat all the candy."
Andrea: "I would not!"
Dale: "Well, then, you would drink all the chocolate milk."
Andrea: "I would not!"
Dale: "Okay, then, you would steal all the money!"

* * *

A group of the boys were involved in a discussion in which they were "yukking" about girls. "I'll never kiss a girl," "I'm never going to get married," and similar rash vows.

But Josie had a word of wisdom for them: "That's all right. You'll change your mind and get married. And you'll get used to kissing!"

* * *

Terry: "My mama is coming home from the hospital today."

Arlene: "Why is your mama in the hospital? Did she have a baby?"

Terry: "No, of course not! Don't be silly! She's not old enough for that!"

* * *

Elaine kept staring at a new boy in the class. I heard her ask herself, "Now why does he look so familiar?" Then after a few moments of deep concentration: "Oh, yeah, I remember, he's my cousin!"

* * *

When Kim and Beth emerged from the housekeeping center royally decked out in all the finery of the dress-up clothes, Scott stared at them and asked, "What are you supposed to be?"

"Oh," they replied, "We're playing 'poor white trash'!"

* * *

Graffiti is not usually a problem with kindergartners, but on the wall in the passageway to the playground someone had written "Jimmy." Some of the children were loitering on the patio, so Donnie pointed to the graffiti and demanded of the others, "Don't you boys know what that says? It says, 'Don't Play Here.' Now get out there to the playground to play."

* * *

The children were doing a color-word worksheet when Lenny, an Afro-American boy, asked a neighbor, "What does this word say?"

Instead of telling him outright, Johnny offered him a hint, "Well, what color are you, Lenny?"

Lenny replied, "I'm brown."

Johnny said, "Oh, that's right. You used to be black, but now you're brown. Well, the word says black."

* * *

Gary: "How do you like your new dad?"
David (shrugging): "Not very much. He yells at me."
Gary: "I know. I had him for a dad last year!"

Chapter 35

Teacher's Pet

"Teacher's Pet" is a perennial taunt thrown at a student who may, or may not, be a favorite with the teacher. In spite of the rule that teachers must not have pets, being only human, they can't help responding more favorably to some of their students, although they try to never show partiality. For that matter, teachers even have favorite classes too, because each class has its own personality, just as much as individuals do.

Not long ago an adult in conversation mentioned school difficulties she had encountered, and how the "smart students were always the teacher's pets." From my own experiences, since I have been both a student and a teacher and even a teacher's pet, I can't agree with her. Teachers may, deep inside, feel a partiality to certain students, but what determines which ones?

Is it the most intelligent? Not necessarily. Sure, it's nice to have smart students; it makes the teacher look good, makes her work easier up to a point. After that, she does double work, trying to keep the smart student interested and challenged. On the other hand, a superior student may become lazy and unmotivated, and use his ability to figure new ways to be annoying.

Is it the best behaved child who becomes a teachers' pet? Not necessarily. A child whose behavior is "perfect" may just blend in until he becomes invisible. Frankly, I always worried about the "model child." There is something abnormal about being that good.

Are teachers more attracted to the most socially adept child? Manners do help, especially if there is some real sincerity behind them. But if the child is merely sociable, that usually means he would rather talk than do lessons.

Is it the prettiest or the handsomest one who wins the distinction of being teacher's favorite child? No one objects to a child being attractive, but the old adage, "Pretty is as pretty does," is as true today as ever.

Will the class comic become the favorite student? It depends on how the miniature comedian uses his wit. Does he use it to enliven an otherwise dull or tense moment, or is it strictly an attention-getting mechanism?

How about the child of: (a) a school board member; (b) the principal; (c) the town's most influential citizen; (d) your best friend? Will any of them become the teacher's pet? Not necessarily, although in some situations one may be inclined to wear kid gloves every day.

Who, then, becomes the teacher's pet? First, none of the above are excluded; they just don't make it home free. Teachers can't help favoring, not necessarily the most intelligent child, but one who is willing to put his best effort into his work, or one who is developing socially and emotionally as well as mentally. The process of maturing doesn't give the child much time to misbehave, or to try to be the class entertainer, or to be unduly concerned about being beautiful. And most small children seem unaware of family connections or position. Older ones are, but most will play it down; a few will try to capitalize on it.

So, who does become the teacher's pet? Intelligence and pleasant behavior help, as do social graces and a sense of humor. Good looks or family position never hurt a child, unless he decides that is all that it takes. The child who sees and respects the teacher as a person rather than as just a school fixture rates high. But in the final analysis, a lot depends on something else not mentioned: personality interaction. And this is something that is totally unpredictable and unintentional.

I have had many, many favorite students and very, very few that I didn't like. Even the obnoxious child has his good points. But I don't believe I ever truly had a pet. I certainly tried not to show any partiality. Actually, anytime I felt that a child was a persona non grata I probably bent over backward to be extra nice to that one. I would never want to hurt a child by making him feel unloved. Showing that child favor often helps correct whatever fault created a feeling of disfavor, be it with me, or with his classmates.

I remember Kip, and there have been others like him, not an "unfavorite" with me, but a child that the other children didn't care for. An inept child that the others considered a dummy even in kindergarten. I made it a point to have Kip's week as Helper arrive as soon as possible. (Helper is the one who takes the attendance slips to the office each day, and does other errands occasionally.) Kip was so shy and insecure that I had to send another child with him the first day, a helper for the Helper, so to speak. But after that he could handle it himself. And I made a big deal of what a good helper he was. This gave him instant esteem in the eyes of the other children and started him in the direction of building some self-esteem.

Who were some for whom I felt special favor? There was Kevin who had figured out reading before he started kindergarten, and who, at free activity time, would sometimes select a book and sit down to read it aloud to any who cared to listen. Sometimes the whole class would be gathered to listen to the story he was reading. I've have had other readers in kindergarten who wouldn't *think* of reading to other children; that was simply beneath them!

Then there was Diana, only mildly pretty, who had to work to stay with the middle reading group in first grade, but she had a real talent for social smoothness. This was rather surprising since she was from a home where striving for the necessities took precedence over social graces. But she demonstrated exceptional skill for saying the right thing, and especially for smoothing over someone else's *faux pas.*

In the same class, there was Jan, a beautiful child with dark hair, blue eyes, and very fair complexion. Jan was brighter than Diana, but a total scatterbrain with a knack for foot-in-mouth. I remember the day during music period when we were joined by Mrs. H.'s class. Mrs. H. must have had a headache, or perhaps her eyes were tired. At any rate, she took off her glasses, laid them on the piano, and rubbed her eyes. Jan said, "Quick, Mrs. H., put your glasses back on. You look like a witch!"

Diana, ever the one to smooth things over, said, "Now, Jan, you don't mean that. She doesn't look like a witch. She just looks different."

"Oh, yeah," said Jan, "that's what I meant. Mrs. H. just looks like a different girl."

(Of course, Mrs. H. forgave her. After all, she was about sixty, and Jan had said she looked like a different *girl!*)

And, of course, Jan charmed me; she was the unintentional entertainer.

Shirley was a year older than her classmates, and very average in ability, but the extra age gave her a definite advantage in maturity. Remember *Dick and Jane*[14] books? The little stories usually had a humorous side to them which the less mature pupils, even the best readers, often missed. But Shirley always caught the humor. She would begin with a giggle that would then explode. This was the cue for the others in her group to take another look at the situation pictured in the story. Then they would see the humor and everyone would have a good laugh. She made my "middle" reading group delightful and lots more fun than my "top" group.

Those are just a few examples of the ways children can earn a special place in the teacher's heart, but in reality, each one is special in his own way.

How can you identify a teacher's pet? Be careful here. You

might misread the signs. I remember other teachers remarking how Mike was Mrs. B.'s pet. They *knew* because she chose him to do all the errands such as take notes to the office. But I knew something different. Mike was a genius-level child whom Mrs. B. hadn't been completely successful in motivating. She had confided to me that it made for a much calmer classroom to have Mike out doing errands as much as possible.

David was a bright child in my first-grade class, quick to grasp and retain whatever was presented. He was not necessarily the very brightest in the class, but definitely top group material. At that time, beginning with second grade, our school had homogeneous grouping. When class assignments for next year were posted, much to my surprise, David was assigned to a middle group even though I had rated him for a high group. I later learned that my supervisor had thought he was my pet, that I had overgraded him because his mother and I were good friends.

Her mistake brought some very undesirable results. David was enough brighter than his classmates that they developed the attitude of, "Ask David. He will know, and we don't. Why bother to try?" David developed an inflated opinion of his own abilities. He needed to be with other children of his ability level to keep things in proper perspective.

(I have always resented a supervisor thinking I would overgrade a child because his parents were my friends. That, after all, would be a very unkind thing to do. Consider how devastating it would be to find yourself in a group where you were totally outclassed just because a teacher had overrated you for whatever reason. You don't do that to your friend's child, or even to your enemy's.)

More about identifying teachers pets. It isn't necessarily the one she calls on most often. That's most likely the arm-waver, the one who raises his hand most enthusiastically to recite, especially if the others are slower to respond. Perhaps she calls on the one whose attention tends to wander. It isn't necessarily the one who brings teacher apples, or flowers, or an interesting rock, or whatever else the class deems to be the proper memento to bring the teacher.

I will interject here a bit about the opposite of teacher's pet, the child that a teacher doesn't like. You know, "Miss Jones isn't fair. She flunked Johnny just because she doesn't like him." Think about it. If a teacher really doesn't like Johnny, does she want him in her class again, a year older and meaner/dumber/smellier, or whatever her complaint is? Not at all. If she really doesn't like him, she will go to all lengths to promote him. Plain logic.

So, who is teacher's pet? Perhaps it is easier to say who is *not* her pet:

The disrespectful child.

The selfish, self-centered child.

The "mouthy" child who hasn't been taught self-control.

The unkind child who hasn't learned to respect the feelings of others.

The dirty child. (Parents' fault. A teacher may feel sorry for the child, but a dirty, smelly child seldom has a chance at being a favorite.)

The child who continually contradicts the teacher or tries to put her down. I could never figure out how a child could become so adept at these things by age five or six. This is a guaranteed way for a child to be an "unfavorite."

So, who *is* teacher's pet? I would say that all those who are kind, respectful, considerate of others, and cooperative, are pets, whether they know it or not. Have I had any pets? Only a few thousand!

Chapter 36

He Grew Germs Off Us

When the kindergarten classes were learning about community helpers we made the study more meaningful by visiting the office of a local doctor for a behind-the-scenes view. One thing that especially impressed the children was having a lab technician actually "grow" some germs he found on the skin of the students by touching them with a cotton swab and inoculating a sterile petri dish, which was then incubated overnight. Some children referred to their germs as "worms." Here are some of their comments taken from their "homework assignment"—a report recorded by a parent "secretary."

* * *

"Mama, guess what! We went on a field trip to a doctor's office. It wasn't the one we go to, but she was nice anyway. She got a stick that was real sharp and got some dirt out of my fingernail. It was germs, and she put it in a kinda box that was red in the bottom to find out what kind of germs we got. It has to stay in the box three days. Georgina got a stick with cotton on it in her mouth to check her germs, and Bill had a stick with cotton on up his nose to get some of their germs to make 'em grow."

* * *

"She rubbed some stuff on us to get all the worms out."

* * *

"The nurse chose John to be the patient. We pretended like John said, 'I got a stomachache, an earache, and a tongueache.' We taked his blood pressure, and we taked his temperature and looked in his mouth. The nurse checked his stomach and said his heart was beating 200."

"The nurse let Ricky listen to his heartbeat. She looked in some kids' mouths and they had to say *ah-h-h-h*. Mrs. Chambers said, 'Dana has a listening problem.' The nurse looked in her ear and said, 'Oh, she has a cherry tree growing there!'"

* * *

"We went to the stitchin' room where they stitch up people."

* * *

"We went to the 'hospital.' Want to hear more about it? Well, we saw some germs, except they looked like they were big because we looked through a microscope. Want me to tell you some more about it? We saw a skeleton. Saw some little thingees in a jar. And I learned about germs. You have to wash your hands before you eat."

"In the medicine room there were better medicines, help medicines, pain medicines, and a 'figerator to put the medicines in so people can get better. Looked in a microscope and saw some really sick germs."

* * *

"We looked at something like water through a 'telescope.' We got to see germs. They looked kinda like grapes."

* * *

"We saw a skeleton, and I told Glen I had one just like it, but mine doesn't have numbers on it. Saw nurses. Saw pictures of some bones, real ugly bones!"

* * *

"I heard my stomach and it sounded like a dog pound. We saw what your heart looks like. It doesn't look like a valentine!

"There were no men there, so I guess the doctor was at the hospital helping some lady get a baby."

***

"I like bacteria 'cause there is good bacteria and bad bacteria."

***

"The bones looked white and soggy. How come your bones look so soggy?"

***

"The nurse showed us a skeleton. A *real* skeleton, except it was plastic. It wasn't tooken out of anybody. And we got to touch it. Then the doctor came in and said about the skeleton, 'Did the nurse introduce you to my mother?'"

***

"They showed us one of those microscope things. It had little balls under it. They said it was blood, but it didn't look like blood to me."

***

"We saw a 'microphone' when the doctor was looking through it. We saw these things connected to the ears and another hose that makes your heart beat.

"The doctor put some stuff on me, and we are going to plant the germs. And I didn't even cry when he put that medicine on me, but my stomach was scared."

***

So, as you can see, the children have their own way of telling what they learned, but on the whole, they gathered a lot of accurate information. And any future trip to the doctor should have been faced with much less apprehension.

Chapter 37

Thank You for This Feud

Everybody has some kind of religious belief, whether he thinks so or not. Hence, all children receive some kind of religious training. For some it is a positive attitude toward spiritual things; for others, it's negative. There is no middle ground. Each child's attitude and beliefs will, from time to time, show through in other settings—as at school. I'm sharing with you a few choice items that came my way.

* * *

The Sunday school teacher had taught her class to recite "The Lord's Prayer," or so she thought until she heard little Glynda's version of "forgive us our trespasses." It was, "Give us this truck passing."

* * *

Shortly before Easter I overheard this conversation between two of my kindergartners:
Pat: "Hey, Doug, what are you giving up for Lent?"
Doug: "I don't know. What are you giving up?"
Pat: "I've decided to give up women—all except my mom."
Doug: "Well, I think I should give up golf."

* * *

163

Little Betsy had faithfully attended baptism classes. On the morning she was to be baptized, her mother, wanting to be sure Betsy understood the significance of this ritual, asked her, "Now, honey, tell me again, what does baptism mean? What does it do?"

Betsy replied, "Well, it isn't the water that makes you clean …."

Mother thought, *Yes, she understands.*

Then Betsy finished, "…it's the soap."

* * *

When Margaret noticed the day moon in the sky, she announced that "God is going to punish the moon for coming out when it's not supposed to."

* * *

Jean probably grew up to be a public relations agent. She told me, "Mrs. Chambers, you should come to my daddy's church. He preaches real good, and his sermons aren't too long."

* * *

Mark informed us, "Jesus has good lions up on the moon where he lives."

* * *

Kindergartners Hank and Michelle had been "engaged," but it seemed that Hank was wanting out of that commitment. Hank told her for about the tenth time, "No, I'm *not* going to marry you."

Finally Michelle said, "Well, that's okay. It doesn't matter. Just because I don't get married doesn't mean I'll go to hell. I can still go to heaven even if I never get married!"

* * *

I was explaining to the children why our floors at school were always warm, that our room was heated by hot water being circulated through copper tubing in the floors. One child asked where the hot water came from. Boyd piped up, "I know, I know! It's from the devil!"

* * *

Shelley was whispering to Howard, and Bill was feeling left out.
Bill: "It's not nice to tell secrets."
Shelley: "We can tell secrets if we want to."
Bill: "Well, it's not nice, and I'll tell God you did it."
Shelley: "That's okay. He already knows!"

* * *

Carmen learned to pray almost as soon as she could talk, and she especially liked to ask the blessing at the table. But she sometimes modified her prayer according to what she would like there to be on the table, as in, "God is great, God is good, and we thank Him for these…potato chips."

When she was about five her mother began teaching her the correct way to answer the telephone, but she sometimes got that a little confused. One day when the phone rang, Mom nodded permission for Carmen to answer it. So Carmen lifted the phone from the hook and, in her best telephone manner answered, "Dear Heavenly Father…"

* * *

My children both liked to ask the blessing, and there was usually a little rivalry as to whose turn it was. If Kathleen won, we could expect to hear "Thank you, Jesus, for this food. I get the biggest piece!…Oh, uh, Amen."

On the other hand, when Benny got to say the blessing, it usually came out, "Thank, you, Jesus, for this *feud*. Amen."

* * *

Some children are confused by the variety of Christian churches. (Some adults are, too.) We were taking a walking field trip. As we passed the Assembly of God church, I heard Jenny say, "I've been to that church. That's where the sinners go to church. I know, 'cause it's called the 'Sinbly.'"

And then as we passed the Baptist church, Helen informed us, "They call that the *Baddest* church 'cause that's where the baddest people go."

* * *

* * *

A child's actions sometimes reveal the extent to which religion is actually practiced in the home.

Little Polly and Jimmy were madly "in love," and they liked to have their rest mats adjacent at rest time. This was all right with me since they were "good resters." On this particular day something had really upset me to the point that I was definitely a grouchy teacher. When nap time came Polly and Jimmy again managed to get their rest mats side by side. Jimmy quickly flopped on his, but Polly said, "No, Jimmy, we have to say our prayers before we lie down."

So Jimmy and Polly each knelt at the foot of their mats. Jimmy mumbled for maybe ten seconds and again flopped on his mat. But not Polly. With closed eyes and folded hands, she prayed and prayed and prayed...and prayed some more before finally lying down. I wanted so much to be able to get near enough to eavesdrop, but I couldn't. Nevertheless, I was so amused that my grouchiness evaporated. I wondered if she had been praying for her teacher's disposition to improve.

* * *

Todd was everything that anyone could ask for in a kindergarten child, cute, smart, well behaved; a real class favorite. When his mother and a friend picked him up at noon that December day, little did anyone dream that we would never see Todd again. But within fifteen minutes they were involved in a traffic accident and Todd and his little sister were instantly killed.

Facing my class the next morning was one of my most heart-wrenching experiences. Five-year-olds have no real understanding of death. Many times on TV they see someone "killed" on one program, and the next day they see the same actor very much alive on another program. The permanence of death is not portrayed.

Of course, they all wanted to talk about it—was he really dead? What did that mean? When would he be back?

I had to explain, "No, Todd will never be in our class again.

We will miss him very much; he was a good friend that we all liked very much. Yes, we feel sad; perhaps you feel like crying. But remember, the Bible tells us that Jesus loves all little children. When little children die they go to live in heaven with Jesus. That is where Todd is now, in heaven where he will always be happy and nothing will ever hurt him or make him sad. Yes, *we* feel sad for ourselves because we will miss him, but Todd is happy where he is."

The children were able to accept this; it was a word of hope for them, and gladness that Todd was not in a hospital somewhere in great pain. I suppose some people would scream that I was teaching religion, and I was. But in my opinion, the hope that the Bible teaches is far more to be desired, and far better emotionally and psychologically, than the hopelessness of death as annihilation and nothingness.

My class handled the loss far better than the children in the other kindergarten class whose teacher told them, "Yes, Todd was killed, but we are *not* going to talk about it, so just hush." (She herself told me that was what she had said.) That could only leave the children feeling that death was an unspeakable dread and shame—no hope, only a deeply negative nothingness.

* * *

More on the subject of death: Many people try to shield their children from any knowledge of death, which is unrealistic considering the violence portrayed on TV. But I'm speaking of natural death. An incident in our family convinced me that a child can deal with death if the adults around him can. Our son, Benny, was seven when my husband's mother died. She was his "nearby" grandmother and as a preschooler he had frequently spent the day at her house instead of going to the babysitter.

She died very suddenly so there was no chance to prepare Benny and Kathleen for the loss. We planned to take them to the funeral, but a relative said, "Oh, no. That's too traumatic for small children. Let's get a babysitter for all the younger ones."

So we did.

Later Benny asked questions like, "What did they do with Grandma? Did they just bury her in the dirt like we did Fido when he died?" We explained that they had put her in a nice big box that was all padded and soft, and we thought this satisfied him. But a day or two later he asked, "How did they get Grandma in that box? Did they fold her up? Or did they cut her in pieces?"

My husband quickly went to the phone, called the mortuary, and arranged for us to take the children over and let them see some coffins—immediately. Benny felt much better about the whole thing after he saw what a coffin was like. But he could have been spared several days of worry had he been taken to the funeral, or at least to the visitation. Kathleen remembered my father's funeral when she was seven, so she was spared the worries that bothered Benny.

Trying to shield a child from any and all association with death is a mistake. I know a child who worried for weeks about his injured cat that "disappeared." His mother, in a mistaken attempt at kindness, had told him it had probably gotten well and run away. He was worried sick that the cat was hungry, or cold, or sick, or would never come home, which, of course, it didn't. When he finally realized the cat had died, he greatly resented that he had been told a lie. Death is a part of life, and if we as adults can accept that, so can our children.

* * *

One more word about religion and our public schools. Teachers have become very cautious about telling the story of the birth of Christ, which is a historical fact. Is history being denied or rewritten? We can no longer have stories of the Old Testament heroes in our readers, but it is all right to have Greek mythology, fairy tales and Native American folk tales. It seems to me that those who believe in freedom *from* religion, not freedom *of* religion, as our Constitution guarantees, have tried to push their atheistic religion on the rest of us.

Chapter 38

Show and Tell

Show and Tell, I found, is best limited to once a week, with exceptions made when it is something that won't wait until next the specified day. The most difficult part to get across to kindergartners is the *tell* part. Most just want to stand in front of the class and hold up an object without saying a word. I insisted that they be able to tell something about it, even if only to say "it is a rock I found on the way to school."

Incidentally, rocks were one of the most popular things to show, followed by "This is the picture I drew," and "This is my new (or favorite)...whatever." However, occasionally a child had something of unusual interest to show or to tell about. A few were unique and stuck in my memory.

* * *

Paul reported, "See this cut on my hand and my skinned elbow? I was riding my bike yesterday evening and I got hit by a car. He didn't even stop 'cause he was running from the police. These are all the hurts I got, but it wrecked my bicycle and bent the wheels and ruined the frame. It broke everything. It *even broke my bicycle bell!*"

* * *

"My mom couldn't find the comb to fix my hair this morning, so you want know what she did? She just combed my hair with a dinner fork!"

* * *

Sometimes the reports were a little too graphic for polite conversation. Billy told us, "My daddy has a horse, and it got sick, and it just poo-pooed all over Grandma's yard. He had to call the vet, and the vet gave the horse a shot with a great big needle. And my grandma is really mad at Daddy 'cause his horse poo-pooed all over her yard. She says *he* has to clean it up."

* * *

Larry brought a nice big picture of a roadrunner, a western bird, for Show and Tell. In his slow, deliberate way, he gave a very nice, obviously practiced speech telling us a great deal about roadrunners—their diet, nesting habits, number of eggs, et cetera. Then he seemed a little unsure about how to end his speech. But he came through with his own conclusion: "And on my daddy's ranch we have, uh— my daddy has two thousand head of roadrunners on our ranch!"

* * *

Another Show and Tell incident which I will never forget happened this way: A classroom rule was if a child needed to use the restroom he/she would quietly get up and go. They were not to interrupt by asking permission or calling attention to themselves. Each room had its own restrooms that opened from the classroom.

During our phonics lesson I was aware that one girl had been to the restroom and returned, then the next girl did likewise, all very decorously, without detracting from the lesson. When a third girl left and then returned, I noticed that she tapped another girl on the shoulder. This girl then went to the restroom, and as she returned she whispered to the next, who also went to the restroom. Something was going on. "Why is it," I asked, "that suddenly every girl has to go to the restroom?"

Someone said, "Jane said for me to tell Suzie to go in there." Then I realized that Jane had not been in her seat for several minutes; in fact, not since the parade to the restroom began. I went to see what the attraction was.

Well, Jane was having her own private Show and Tell for girls only. With a new baby at Jane's house she had been feeling left out. So, in order to show Jane that she, too, was special, and to help her assume the role of big sister, the wise mother had bought Jane new undies, and I mean *fancy*! Ruffles across the fanny, *and* a little *bra* to match! Only a big sister could have all that!

What did I do? I returned to the class and said, "All right, all the girls who haven't had a turn, please come now. We'll have Jane's Show and Tell. No, boys, it's not for you!"

* * *

My daughter Kathleen's first-grade teacher came to me laughing about Kathleen's contribution to Show and Tell. "Last week the Dairy Queen opened. And do you know who's running it? My daddy's girlfriend!"

Now in our small town that could start a real scandal. But the real reason her teacher got such a laugh out of the announcement was that *her* husband also spoke of the Dairy Queen proprietor as *his* girlfriend, and for the same reason that mine did. They each thought they got the largest milkshake in town!

* * *

Little Pedro reported one morning, "Teacher, guess what! I found a rattlesnake in my yard. I called my daddy, and he spanked it on the head 'til it died!"

* * *

Carlos told us, "You know my brother's neck? He fell in the river up to it."

* * *

The absolute worst time for Show and Tell is right after Christmas when too many children want to tell, not only every single thing they received, but also, what every other member of their thing they received, but also, what every other member of their family got. This is especially bad when some others are sitting quietly and looking sad, and you can guess what Christmas was like at those homes. My method on the first day of school after the holidays was to let each child name one, and *only one*, gift. This saved the feelings of poorer children or of any who might not celebrate Christmas at all. It also saved a lot of time.

* * *

And then there was Wally who said, "Hey, look! I got something here I want to show you!" as he quickly unbuckled his belt and unzipped his pants. No, he wasn't a flasher; Santa had brought him bright red underwear.

Chapter 39

Questions, Pertinent and Impertinent

Questions That Teachers Ask

I was trying to elicit the word "face" from the class. "What does your mother say when she wants you to wash your nose, mouth, and cheeks? What does she say when she wants you to wash this part?" (Indicating the face.)

Jeff said, "My mom says, 'Go wash your mug'."

* * *

Teacher: "Who do we see in this picture?"
Dale: "A mailman."
Teacher: "That's right, but not everyone who works for the post office is a man. Can you think of another name we could use?"
Pat: "Well, we could call them 'mail droppers'."

* * *

The test question was, "When you are asleep your eyes are shut, and when you are awake your eyes are _____."

Bryan promptly answered, "Bloodshot."

* * *

Teacher: "Where does butter come from?"
Lynn: "Butterflies."

* * *

One part of the achievement test given at the close of kindergarten involved picture interpretation. This was Carlos' description of the picture: "Daddy is running. A dog is with Daddy. They have legs, but Daddy has two legs and the dog has four legs. The daddy has shoes, but the dog doesn't. The dog has a curled tail, and the dog's ears are different from the man's. The dog has a stomach, and he walks different to the daddy. And the dog will have babies, but the daddy won't!"

* * *

I was trying to refresh the children's memory on the words of a nursery rhyme song:
"I'm a great big boy,
a great big boy am I,
Very fond of ____, ____." (Candy, very fond of pie.)
But David finished it his way— "*Girls!*"

* * *

And Questions That Children Ask

Scott put his hands over his eyes, then asked, "Who turned out the lights?"

* * *

Leslie wanted to know, "Why do mamas always have grandmas for their mamas?"

* * *

One day my daughter and her husband dropped by my classroom for a moment. I introduced her, "Children, you remember I told you that I had a little girl, but she grew up to be bigger than I am. Well, this is my little girl. Her name is Kathleen, and you can see that she is taller than I. And this is her husband."
And one child asked, "Was he ever a little boy?"

* * *

The mother of one kindergarten student worked in the special education department of our school system. Consequently, little Sara had heard dinner table conversation about "special ed." all her life. After starting to school she asked her mother, "Mom, why does Tommy get to go to school all day while I only get to go half a day?"

"What do you mean, Sara? I don't think any kindergartners go all day."

"Tommy does. Tommy goes to kindergarten with me all morning. And then that man comes and takes him at noon," explained Sara.

Mom responded with a feeling of alarm, just as any of us do in view of horror stories we sometimes hear. "That man? What man? Who do you mean? Who comes and takes Tommy away?"

"Oh, Mom, that man! You know, *That Man*! You talk about him all the time, *That Man*. You know, *Special Ed*!"

* * *

A child delivering a note to a class that had team teachers looked in confusion from one teacher to another, and then to the aide. Finally he asked, "Well, who is the owner here, anyway?"

* * *

Jerry asked, "Isn't it time to go home yet? When we get home from school we've got to go to Safford and get that check. My daddy says that when he gets that check he's going to go get drunk with it."

* * *

Ronnie: "Mrs. Chambers, do you know why I'm all dressed up so pretty? It's so I can catch me some more girlfriends!"

* * *

My four-year-old Benny had a wonderful new toy, a semi-tractor and trailer, an 18-wheeler, which he had personally selected from the Sears catalog. When his cousin, Sandra, a high school senior, dropped in he proudly brought it out to show her. She admired it properly, and then, assuming that we had called his attention to the name on the trailer, she asked him,

"What does it say on the side of your semi?"

He looked at her with a thunderstruck expression and asked, "What's the matter? Can't you read?"

* * *

I was wearing a T-shirt that said, "Be nice to me. I had a hard day." Precocious Eric, a four-year-old who could already read, looked at it, thought for a moment, then asked, "How can you tell this early in the morning?"

Chapter 40

Kate and Dupli-kate

Twins are always fascinating, especially when they are young enough that their actions are not yet affected by what others think twins are supposed to be like. Incorrect use of "the pill" must have increased the incidence of twins in the sixties and early seventies; we had at least one set of twins in kindergarten every year for a while. One year we had *five* sets. Then the number dropped to nearer the usual level; improvement in the use of the pill, I presume.

Twins used to be kept together in the same classroom at school, but in the late fifties it was decided they should be separated, a decision I agree with since there is always a dominant twin that the other one relies on instead of developing his own potential.

We had several sets of identical twins, but I could always learn to tell them apart, at least if I had the two together. It's something about the eyes—a difference in the expression when they look at you. I recall a set of mirror-image twins. All I had to do was watch their actions; the right-handed twin was the one in my class.

A particularly memorable set of twins, from the days before we separated twins, was Robert and Randal, or as they pronounced it, "Wobby" and "Wandy."

They were certainly identical, but I learned to tell them apart by the expression of the eyes. Randy was the dominant twin, and the brighter one. He always grasped the lesson more quickly, his work was better, and his name was written more plainly.

One day at dismissal time one of the twins dashed from the classroom door and ran right into a metal pole that supported the patio roof. I ran over and picked him up; he had a gash above one eye and blood running down his face. As I hurried him around the corner to the nurse's office, I asked, "Which one are you?"

He replied, "I'm Wandy."

The nurse did her first aid thing, and Mom came and took him to the doctor for a few stitches. After that I didn't need to bother looking into their eyes to see which twin it was. Randy was the one with the bandage above the eye, and later on, the scar.

But it seemed as though that little accident must have upset him more than one might expect. His school work just never was as good as previously; but at the same time Robby's improved considerably. Well, sometimes a child makes a sudden spurt of progress.

Then, on the last day of school, when Mom came to pick up the boys, I remarked that Randy's accident had made it easy to tell at a glance which twin was which. She said, "But it wasn't Randy. Robby is the one with the scar!"

That little rascal! With the pain of the cut and the blood running down his face, he had, for who knows what reason, given me his twin's name. And from then on, they had swapped seats in the classroom. Robby, who had had difficulty learning to write his own name, from then on wrote *Randy* on his papers, and vice versa. Well, certainly the smarter twin had not done himself a favor by trading identities with his brother. Who would have thought that five-year-olds would have carried on the deception for two months?

* * *

A couple who lived on an isolated ranch in our area had twins. They felt that it was a mistake to make a big deal out of the twinship, thus the girls got the idea that babies always came in pairs. But then they had triplets, which really upset the twins. They didn't know what should be done with the extra baby.

* * *

Another set of twins, cute little boys, but not identical, were very easy to tell apart. Nevertheless, one morning Larry bopped into my room and asked, "Do you know which twin I am?" Then he proceeded to answer his own question before I could: "I'm the beautiful one!" He was right. All young children are beautiful.

Chapter 41

Love Offerings

The apple is often used as a symbol of a child's admiration, sometimes even adoration, of his teacher, or sometimes as a bribe for a good grade as in "polish the apple." Yes, I've received a good many apples, usually edible red ones, some of which had been taste-tested by the giver. I have also received grapes that barely survived the trip to school, oranges, pears, and pecans. Also cookies and homemade fudge; usually carefully wrapped in saran wrap or in a plastic sandwich bag, but sometimes offered from grubby little hands.

At Christmas I have received the whole range of gifts, about the same as any elementary school teacher would get. But kindergarten and first grade teachers frequently have love offerings bestowed upon them that teachers of older children would never be blessed with. This varies from year to year. Some years it would be autumn leaves or things from nature; perhaps a bird feather or the shed skin of a snake. Rocks were a popular gift. Some years I received *lots* of rocks; interesting, remarkable, or otherwise. One year so many rocks accumulated that I purchased special craft glue and had the children glue rocks together and add movable eyes to create "rock critters."

I have received a few unique love offerings that remain remarkably fresh in my mind, not because of the value of the gifts, but for the spirit in which they were given.

* * *

I remember Ron who came in with a box containing a jar of jelly. "Hey, Teacher, I brought you some prickly pear jelly that my mom made. And it doesn't have any stickers in it!" Delicious! And he was right, there were no stickers!

* * *

Little Sidney bounced into the classroom with a proud smile early one morning. "Mrs. Chambers, I've got something for you. I want to give you some money." And he laid a fistful of bills on my desk; twenties, I believe they were. I started to remonstrate, but then a quick glance told me "play money." I thanked him and left the *money* on my desk. Just then my aide, Mrs. E., walked in, so Sidney also gave her a handful of his money, and then went to the playground.

At the end of the day, Mrs. E. and I gave the *money* another casual glance. It looked like factory rejects with creases and pleats in the paper, mostly printed on one side only. So, without even stopping to wonder how Sidney happened to come into possession of factory-rejected play money, it went the way of many of the love offerings bestowed upon us, into the *round file*. Mrs. E. and I had both forgotten about this incident until later in the week when the news media came out with detailed newscasts about Sidney's father being arrested for producing counterfeit money.

* * *

It was approaching Christmas, and a number of children had brought beautifully wrapped little packages and announced, "This is for you, Mrs. Chambers," as they put them under our Christmas tree.

Then, on the last day little Jim (who was from a very poor family, and who never did learn to say my name right) came in all smiles with his gift. "Hey, 'Missin Changers,' I brung you a present, and I wrapped it all by myself!" (That was obvious.)

Like so many children, he wanted me to open it immediately, but there wasn't time right then. Later, after our party was over and the last child had departed, I opened my gifts. When I opened the one from Jim I was both amazed and amused. He had not only wrapped it himself; he had certainly selected it himself, from the family medicine cabinet. It was a disposable razor, no doubt from Daddy's supply. At least it was new — I think. I had fun writing him a thankyou note mentioning the usefulness of the gift and his thoughtfulness, but making sure *not* to say what the gift was. Let the parents find out from him.

* * *

This might be entitled "The Gift I Didn't Get." Little Rodney's family had relatives in Flagstaff, where it snows a lot. That's where they always went for holidays. Flagstaff is about a six-hour drive from Willcox, through Tucson and Phoenix, both noted for their mild winter weather.

After Christmas vacation Rodney informed me, "I had a present for you, but Mom wouldn't let me bring it. I had to leave it at Grandma's in Flagstaff. It was a box full of snowballs."

Chapter 42

So Who Is Handicapped?

The dictionary defines "handicap" as any disadvantage that makes achievement or success difficult. We often think of handicaps as being physical, and sometimes they are, but let's take a look at some real children and decide which ones have problems that have been allowed to become real handicaps.

Sandy was born with malformed hands — she had no thumbs. When her mother brought her on the opening day of school she quietly mentioned to me that Sandy had no thumbs, then added emphatically, "But she is *not* handicapped. She can do anything that any of the others can do." And she was right. Sandy could operate scissors with perfect ease; she could even tie her own shoes.

Bobby was a happy, outgoing child who enjoyed lots of rough-and-tumble play at recess in spite of a withered arm. I'm sure he realized that he would never be a basketball star, but he didn't let a crippled arm hamper his spirit.

Pedro was an albino Mexican child. The Anglo children resented his not speaking English, and the Mexican kids resented this "Anglo who tried to be Mexican."

Billy was able to do almost none of the things expected of a kindergartner. He preferred to roll around on the floor like a baby and would actually have liked a bottle. Billy was definitely a retarded child who needed special education, but that was before public schools were able to provide it.

Mark was unable to do any first-grade work, not even reading readiness. He spent his time moving around the room studying each bulletin board at length, and interrupting my reading groups with questions about what he saw. The next day he asked the same questions again, and again. But he knew every teacher in the school by name. Within a year or so he became violent and was diagnosed as schizophrenic, so yes, he had a real handicap.

Tiffany had an attitude problem and a smart mouth. Did that make her handicapped? Yes, and needlessly so. While I don't know the cause of her attitude problem, it was likely rooted in her home life as she had the problem from the first day of kindergarten on. The smart mouth problem indicated a lack of parental control and training and was a real social handicap for the child.

Susie always complained, "Nobody will play with me." What she meant was that the most popular child in the class didn't select her for an exclusive friend. Susie refused the option of making friends and playing with a "left-out" child (left out because of shyness) who would have welcomed Susie's friendship. Susie was spoiled and self-centered. Another *socially* handicapped child.

Dell would invariably come crying and tattling, "Johnny hit me back!" He was handicapped by being over-indulged and under-disciplined. His mother said she had taught him that it wasn't nice to hit back. I guess she forgot to teach him that it wasn't nice to hit *first*, either. The last I heard of Dell he was on his way to prison for grand theft, and assault and battery.

Sarah wore two hearing aids, but still missed a lot of the lessons in spite of the teacher's efforts to be sure she heard. Certainly this was a handicap, but she bravely made the best of it, never letting it spoil her attitude or disposition. She is now married, and has two children with normal hearing, but sadly she is losing her sight.

Ronnie, with severe dyslexia, was doubly handicapped. First, with the dyslexia which was made worse by the fact that I (and teachers in general) didn't know how to help him. Second, and more importantly, by his parents' rejection. I can understand the parents' frustration and bewilderment over the disorder, but not their attitude toward the child.

Gina seemed very lost in kindergarten and made very little progress. She was able to write only the first letter of her name (and backward at that) by the end of the school year. She was probably on the low side of normal intelligence, but she was soon labeled a "slow learner." Her problem, which we learned much too late, was that she was too young for kindergarten. There were more little ones at home and Gina was tall for her age, so Mom got her out from underfoot by sending her off to school.

This was before schools became strict about birth certificates, and it was my first year teaching kindergarten. With a little more experience I learned to identify the too young, even those who were legally old enough. When the cause of Gina's backwardness was discovered two years later she was already hopelessly turned off toward school.

Brenda never had enough energy to do much school work. She was too tired to learn to read. Quite by accident I learned that Brenda ate no breakfast. Her mother's breakfast, she told me, was coffee and a cigarette. I convinced Brenda that she could fix herself a piece of toast and a bowl of cold cereal. When she ate breakfast she performed satisfactorily at school, but she evidently got no encouragement on the breakfast bit at home. I had to remind her periodically about the importance of eating breakfast. I could always tell when she had skipped eating. Perhaps she could be classified as handicapped by parental neglect.

Robert had so many changes of parents that he didn't know which were his real parents or who he was. However, in spite of the serial parents, he seemed to find himself, probably because of the one stable person in his life, his grandmother. He starred in sports in high school. I'm sure he has emotional scars from his checkered childhood, but he seems to function satisfactorily in spite of it.

Charlie was a dwarf— 27 inches tall in kindergarten, where the average height is 45 inches. People, even other kindergartners, were inclined to treat him like a doll. I tried to keep that to a minimum by making special arrangements to accommodate him, such as a step stool in the boys' rest room so he could reach the light switch and the toilet without assistance. He grew a little in the first grade, but his vision began to fail, and the following year he had to go to the School for the Deaf and Blind in Tucson. Yes, Charlie had some handicaps, but he handled them well.

Debbie cried whenever she made a mistake, or even thought she had. Debbie had to learn that everybody makes mistakes, and the teacher isn't going to eat you alive if you do. Even teachers make mistakes, and I always told the children that I didn't allow any perfect people in my class; only children who sometimes made mistakes were allowed in.

Jerry had trained himself to regurgitate any time he didn't like the taste of a food. This resulted in his being denied snacks in kindergarten and barred from the cafeteria in first grade. He was definitely handicapped emotionally and socially. I hope he eventually broke himself of the vomiting habit. If not, picture him at eighteen taking his girlfriend out to dinner.

Paula lived with her grandmother as her mother was in prison for child abuse. She had witnessed her little brother being scalded to death by their mother. There is no doubt that the experience scarred little Paula for life and contributed to some of the dysfunctional areas in her abilities.

Jill thought that school was an *a la carte* thing; do only the assignments that are easy or suit your fancy. She hadn't leaned that we all have to do some things we don't like. It's called self-discipline. Sometimes it's called growing up.

Mary was sensitive. She knew because her mother said so. More often than not, she was sad or hurt and in tears, even though her mother had told the teacher that people musn't hurt Mary's feelings. It's too bad that while Mom was telling Mary how sensitive she was that she didn't also tell her to be more sensitive to the feelings of others. Is she handicapped? Probably.

And then there was **Sheila** who was blind in one eye. This might not have been immediately obvious, except that the normal eye was brown and the blind eye was a faded blue.

School had already started before Sheila's mother brought her to my classroom after school so we could get acquainted. She was a lovely child, perfect features and beautiful coloring. Sheila was aware of her difference, but her family had handled the situation wisely, and she accepted it as "just the way it is."

I wondered how the other children would react, and how soon it would be commented on by some child. I also wondered just how it should be handled when the inevitable happened. I didn't have to wait long, as about the third day after Sheila entered the class another child said, "Sheila looks funny with one brown eye and one blue eye." I thought, "Sheila has dealt with this all her life and is an intelligent, well-adjusted child. I'm sure she can handle it." So I turned to her and said, "Sheila, would you like to tell the children about your eyes?"

Her poise and dignity were beautiful. She stepped to the front, faced the class, and said, "The reason my eyes are not the same color is because I'm blind in the blue eye. When I was a baby an accident happened to me and made me blind in that eye. My mother says it just made her sick when my blind eye turned blue. When I get older I will wear a contact lens in that eye so it will be brown like the other one. But I get along with fine seeing out of just one eye."

Want to hear the rest of that story? No teacher with thirty-five first graders is thrilled at being told, "You're getting another child in your class today." But it happened to me perhaps two weeks after Sheila entered my class. I was thinking, "I don't have room for another child. Where will I seat her? Will I have another set of books for her? We're out of locker space." Of course, you hide your despair from the newcomer, but when **Karen** walked in, I took one look and was elated. Why? Karen, with perfectly normal vision, had one brown eye and one blue eye. One child's comment was, "Well, some people have brown eyes and some have blue eyes, and some get one of each!" With that, the whole class accepted that as the norm.

Karen was with us only a few weeks, but I felt as though she had been heaven-sent. And what became of Sheila? She was valedictorian of her graduating class and went on to become a lawyer. As she said, "I get along fine with seeing out of just one eye."

In thinking about these cases my conclusion has to be that there are many kinds of disabilities that don't have to be handicaps, unless one lets them cripple the spirit. The parents of a child with a disability should avoid being *too* good to the child by doing things for him that he can do for himself, even through his efforts may be crude. A good rule is to never do for a child what he can do for himself. Being able to do things for himself will help build his spirit and self-esteem. Encourage him to do the impossible.

In summary, many children are handicapped by the neglect or failure of parents in the role of parenting, which includes a balance of love, training and discipline. And many children *of all ages* are handicapped by undesirable attitudes. Attitude is the key, both the parents' and the child's.

Chapter 43

Oats, Peas, Beans, And Barley Grow

So says the old nursery rhyme/singing game. However, around Willcox we would need to adjust that list of crops. "Lettuce, maize, beans, and cotton grow" would fit better. Until the early 1950s this area was almost exclusively ranching. Now, in addition to the above-mentioned crops, corn, safflower, grapes, tomatoes, and a variety of vegetables are grown on a commercial scale. And in more recent years apples, pecans, and pistachios have become important crops, but the latest is the ostrich. (Do you suppose that someday cowboys will be replaced by ostrich-boys?)

As part of their social studies we took the kindergarten classes on a number of field trips each year to learn about agricultural and ranching enterprises. This chapter includes comments from some of their reports.

A trip to visit a grain elevator was as educational to teachers and parent volunteers as it was to the children. The concept of that "mountain of stuff" being feed for animals was difficult for some children. In their stories it was referred to as dirt, sand, hay, birdseed, wheat, and a few other imaginative names. And some children still didn't believe that what they saw was an elevator. They expected to see "a little room for people to go up and down in."

They were all fascinated by the scales, especially when they were weighed as a group. One class weighed 2720 pounds, and another weighed 2660 pounds. As one child said in her story, "We stood on a board. It went down to the ditch and up to the highest to pound us."

Other comments and stories were:

"We went to see all the grain. They lifted the trucks up high and they almost tipped over. We got to eat some grain in our classroom. The grain would tickle you if you played in it."

* * *

"The grain goes up a pipe, then it comes down those two holes and makes a big pile. They bring the grain in a dump truck with a door so they can get it out. It's birdseed grain. A truck takes it to the store so people can buy it for their birds. It doesn't itch them because they wear gloves. That's all except that we ate some of the grain. It tasted good, and it won't hurt us. But if any of us fell in that hole, we would be made into birdseed. Did you know that?"

* * *

"Went in a bus with a *1* and an *0* on it — Number 10. This thing pours the hay down to the cows — an elevator to put hay in. They weigh it. It's hay, but in small pieces."

* * *

"Dirt — we saw some dirt. It was itchy. No, not dirt, it was grain. It had colors in it — but not purple. It was in a pile, but we didn't get in it because it was itchy."

* * *

A trip to see a cotton field and to the cotton gin brought these comments:

"We went on a field trip to the cotton gin. It wasn't very far. It took almost all day. I didn't count the miles — maybe about a hundred!" (Actually, 15 miles.)

* * *

"The cotton grows on little bushes that are just a little bit in the ground. If you took the seeds out of the cotton and planted them we would have cotton trees. Little trees."

* * *

"They showed us how a machine works. It was green. They pick cotton with it. There's a thing, an air conditioner, and the cotton goes up through it and then into the big basket. After the cotton is in the green basket they put it in an orange basket. The cotton picker dumped the cotton into the cotton trailer. That basket on the cotton picker — all us kids could fit inside it! It's that big! See how much cotton I've got. I'm going to feed it to our buffalo-horse."

(Buffalo-horse?)

* * *

"We got to see some cotton growing, but we didn't pick any. It bloomed. But there wasn't any bathroom there!"

* * *

"A gin looks like a kind of house. We saw trailers of cotton, and we saw the kind of thing that looks like a vacuum cleaner. It just sucks up the cotton."

* * *

"The cotton is put in bales — not *bells*, like 'jingle', but *bales*. I think the bales are brown and white, not blue. Cotton is used for sore ears, rest mats, and kinda for clothes."

* * *

"Some things went 'round and 'round — that's how the motors run. A man gave us some cotton seeds. They put the cotton in a thing to smash it down. Then they put the cotton in a bag. Then they roll it outside. A man came in a tractor and took it away. We couldn't smoke over there because we would all get on fire."

* * *

"You clean the seeds and pop it into popcorn. That's my own idea."

* * *

"The cotton went into a squashing machine that squashed it into a square. Then it was wrapped in cloth and was put with metal straps on."

* * *

"We had to hold on to the teacher's hands or put our hands in our pockets because there were motors, and it was really cold in there. Know what I'm going to do with these cotton seeds? I'm going to plant them when I grow up. I'm going to raise cotton!"

* * *

As always, the children went home with a generous mixture of information and misinterpretation in their brains. But at least no one thought that *cotton gin* was just another kind of alcoholic drink.

* * *

Visits to observe lettuce harvest gave us some more interesting observations and opinions:

"Got on a bus, went to a country. Saw lettuce fields and milo grain fields, and Mr. McGregor's garden, I think."

* * *

"We saw some guys cut the lettuce up and scrape them up and put them on the ground. And then we saw some men put it in boxes — 24 lettuces in one box. Then a guy would staple them. The guys that stapled them up stacked them in a row. We walked on the lettuce leaves, but we couldn't step on the heads."

* * *

"I seen lettuce, and people picking it. And if it was brown on the bottom they'd throw it down on the ground. Big boxes that were stapled with big pins."

* * *

"We watched them sew the boxes, and we got to see them put the lettuce in the boxes. He filled three heads of lettuce in one box at one time. We saw the man who cut into that lettuce with that big ol' knife and went chomp, chomp, chomp. He was cutting it to put into the boxes."

***

"A man had a finger cut off cuz he wasn't careful cutting lettuce. They picked up the lettuce with one hand, and in the other hand they had a knife and they took one swing like a sword and cut it. And there was this man that could carry 10 boxes. He was strong."

***

"That lettuce was so good I couldn't believe my mouth!"

***

"We looked at tomatoes and salad (lettuce) and carrots. We tried not to step on the lettuce, and we got to eat some lettuce. We got back on the bus, and then my teacher said, 'Ladies and gentlemen, lay your heads back and rest, and we'll be back at school in a minute.' And then we were!"

***

One child came up with this interesting bit of mis-information concerning lettuce that had gone to seed: "If lettuce grows too long it turns into a Christmas tree."

***

Observations from other field trips include:

"We rided on a big bus. When we got there we stopped! The first thing we saw was alfalfa. I wish I had a horse to feed alfalfa to."

***

"We saw chickens, Mom, and eggs! We saw chickens sitting down and they were laying eggs!"

***

"We went on a bus to a cow field. There were no cows there—just cow hay!"

***

"We saw a green plant that horses and cows eat. I think it's called 'alfa'."

***

"Saw pigs from the north and from the south. They were big and ready to butcher, but they weren't butchered yet. One big white pig in a pen all by itself. I'm sure it is a daddy pig."

* * *

"Saw a pig with a giant head and round eyes, like me. Goats and cats. They have a lot of rabbits there and chickens. Kids are baby goats. We saw ducks and gooses. They're really geese."

* * *

"We saw a mommy pig that didn't have any babies. How could it be a mommy? Never saw any kangaroos. Saw a fat mother sheep — no, it was a daddy sheep."

* * *

"We saw the baby goats from the mama goat. One baby, just one — but she's still fat. Is she going to have more babies?"

* * *

"We saw a pig named Petunia. His nose wrinkled when he sniffed. Our noses don't do that. We saw a mother and dad goat, and a baby. They were going to teach him to walk because he was just born last night. The mother and dad goat had to stay up until he got born."

* * *

"Saw a chicken setting in a cage fixing to have a baby chicken."

* * *

"We had to tell the bus driver 'Thank you,', and I said it the loudest. I'm not telling you what we had for snack... milk and cookies. That's all."

Chapter 44

Get Along with *Who*?

I must admit that I didn't learn much in most of the education courses I had in college, but I do remember one bit of wisdom uttered by our professor in a course called teaching of reading, and it had nothing to do with reading. He told us, "Remember, when you start teaching, it's all right to fight with another teacher; it's all right to fight with a parent; it's even all right, sometimes, to fight with your principal. But whatever you do, get along with your janitor, because if you don't, he can make your life miserable!"

It sounded amusing to me at that time, but I have had opportunity through the years to observe this wisdom in action. My first year of teaching was in a little crossroads community in West Texas. Our school building was heated with big old-fashioned coal-burning stoves. Part of our janitor's job was to make the rounds ever so often and check the stoves, adding more coal if needed. It seemed to me that invariably, just as I was nailing down the main point of the lesson, that was when he would come and start rattling the stove and adding more coal. By the time he was through I had lost the attention of my class; the magic moment was gone. Remembering my professor's advice, I never complained. I never felt that it was malicious, for after all, he had about nine or ten stoves to tend. There was no perfect moment to check each one. And since I was cold-natured, I appreciated a warm room.

However, my warm-natured roommate, Annette, fell out of his good graces. She was really a kind, thoughtful person, and very shy. But she had a problem — without meaning to, whenever some mishap befell someone else, she would laugh. Not that she thought the mishap was amusing or that she was glad it happened. It was a nervous reaction that, try as she might, she could not suppress.

The windows in our building opened outward. One day when the janitor was working in a flower bed just outside her open window, he raised up and whacked his back against the window and Annette laughed. Well, her room was on the east and got plenty of morning sunshine, but none in the afternoon. So thereafter, he would roast her classroom with a red hot stove all morning when they already had plenty of solar heat. Then he wasn't seen again the rest of the day, and by mid-afternoon her room felt like a freezer. Whether they are sweltering or shivering, uncomfortable kids are hard to teach. He had his revenge.

This was during World War II, and the armed services were taking all the able-bodied men. As a result, the next year, sometimes we had a janitor, and sometimes we didn't. I remember a time when, for a few weeks, we had some high school boys doing the cleaning. If I had been grading them on their janitorial work, I would have given them about an F-minus. Part of the time the teachers each swept and dusted their own rooms. That helps one learn to really appreciate a good janitor.

Fortunately, during most of my teaching years we had janitors (now called custodians) whose work varied from acceptable to excellent. At various times we have had custodians who did good work, but brought their small children with them, and the children sometimes wreaked havoc. One couple I recall were very conscientious and did good work, but their two children were definitely not a help.

For example, I had a *"Hansel and Gretel"* scene made of cardboard with cut-out figures of the various characters made to stand up. The morning after I set up the scene I found the witch's head had been torn off. I fastened it back on the body with transparent tape, but the next morning she was decapitated again. Once more I restored her head, but the next morning — you guessed it — beheaded once more! This went on for several days, until I finally just put the set away. I didn't mind when their children drew on the chalkboard or even painted at the easel, as long as they didn't put the red brush in the green paint, but I didn't want a child committing witch-abuse in my room.

I recall one other custodian. I usually stayed late after school clearing away the day's work and getting set up for the following day. This custodian, whom we *endured*, insisted on cleaning the students' tables with a strong disinfectant (good idea). Which she applied with a spray bottle (bad idea). It gave me asthma that would go into bronchitis. My requests that she do the other rooms first and come back to mine after I left fell on deaf ears until the principal, tired of paying for substitutes for me, issued an edict that Room 2 would be done last.

By and large, throughout the years I found the professor's advice to be sound. Good janitoring is almost a science. Conscientious, efficient custodians are a vital part of a smoothly operating school system, and a good janitor certainly deserves the utmost respect.

Chapter 45

We Had Fun at the Dentist's Office

A trip to the dentist fills many adults with fear, but after a class visit to the dentist many kindergartners said they thought it was fun. These comments are from their homework reports after a non-threatening visit there.

* * *

"Mom, did you put about the dentist? Put that at the top; that's where we went. Oh yeah, put in that he gave us a toothbrush."

* * *

"We went to the dentist's office. He checked my teeth because I raised my hand. I got to sit in the dentist chair that goes up and down. He said I have new teeth coming in. He let us feel a little vacuum-cleaner-like thing. I got embarrassed in front of all those kids.

"He gave us a little bitty toothbrush. You have to put half of it on the pink. And there is something else—it just takes a little wiggle. He showed us those little hook-on things and they feel the cavity, and the dentist fills it."

* * *

"We saw the pressure cooker to clean things."

* * *

* * *

"I got to see some teeth that looked like chalk. I saw wax teeth or whatever. I learned not to eat too much sweet things, and to eat sugarless gum, I mean."

* * *

"There was a mirror for you to look in your mouth except it would be upside down. And there was an exer-ray, but for the teeth."

* * *

"I saw some teeth that were out. He made them out of teeth he pulled out of people. He made some gums. Do you have any more questions?"

* * *

"He made statues of teeth."

* * *

"Oh, this is good! I saw the dentist working on these teeth for a man, 'cause he lost all his teeth. They were fake ones."

* * *

"Now I have to eat a lot of fruit and drink some milk, but I don't like milk, just chocolate. We got a little toothbrush too, and I have to brush my teeth good all the time. I was going to tell the man to give me those other kind of teeth. What are they called? Oh yes, braces."

* * *

"We seen the doctor's tools. He had some pliers, that's all."

* * *

"They gave us a free toothbrush made of soft leather."

* * *

"Did you know that a cavity is a big hole in a tooth? And everybody has four cavities? I can feel the hole in my teeth. Check yours. Everybody has them. I think Mrs. Chambers is going to be checking teeth now."

(An interesting bit of misinformation.)

* * *

"He showed us a hook thing that takes out cavities."

* * *

"Mommy, I like the dentist. He's nice. He showed us a chair that goes up and down. We saw this little gidget. There's three gidgets. One of them spitted moisture. The next one sucked up the water into a pipe. You get this little pack of film and put it close to your tooth. He gets a machine and takes a picture of the tooth. Then he puts the packet of film in a dark room. It takes two or three minutes to develop."

* * *

"We went to the dentist, and he didn't pull nobody's teeth! He had a big, big toothbrush that wouldn't even go in Dad's mouth! And I need some dental frost to clean my toothache so I won't have any more cavities."

* * *

"A girl had lost some of her teeth and the dentist took something like silly putty or clay to make a model of her teeth."

* * *

"He showed us a thing to pull out your toothache."

* * *

"So there, you see, it didn't hurt a bit."

Chapter 46

Some Things You're Never Prepared For

Giggle, giggle, giggle. The scene was the "brown baggers" section of the school cafeteria, and one little group of first-grade girls was really in high spirits. The lunchroom teacher's shushing had only a momentary effect; soon they were gigglier than ever, really giddy. As the teacher started over to investigate she noticed they were all sharing the contents of Kelly's thermos. A quick check of the thermos revealed the cause; Kelly had fixed her own lunch and had filled her thermos with *wine*. Several parents had to be called to take their slightly inebriated six-year-olds home.

It's good to allow or require a child to prepare his/her own lunch. In fact, in order to raise a self-confident, self-reliant child an adult should never do for Johnny what Johnny can do for himself. Nevertheless, it is wise to check up on Johnny occasionally.

* * *

The boys had been careless about the use of the urinal, and I had had to talk with them about being careful. The next day a boy rushed up and informed me that Johnny was in the rest room wetting on the floor. I went to check on the matter, and the conversation went like this:

Teacher: "Johnny, why did you wet on the floor when the urinal was right there?"

Johnny: "Well, somebody opened the door, and when I turned to see who it was, my thing just turned, too!"

* * *

Some of the things that happen at school are amusing; some are not. It was definitely *not* amusing to have a blasting cap found on our playground. In case you're not familiar with blasting caps, they are the devices used in setting off dynamite, used in mining and such. A blasting cap is extremely explosive if not handled with great care, much more so than the dynamite itself. Since there is some mining and prospecting in this area, a few children do recognize blasting caps, but most do not.

Fortunately, the child who found the blasting cap on the playground knew enough to take it to the office, but for a child to handle one at all is scary. This event led the principal to ask all teachers to talk to their children about the dangers of blasting caps. They were warned that anytime they might see some strange object on the playground, not to touch it, but to report it to the playground teacher.

In my class the children asked, "What is a blasting cap?"

And one child quickly volunteered, "I know. It's the kind of cap that a policeman wears."

* * *

Charming little Gary bounced into my kindergarten room before class one morning and asked, "Mrs. Chambers, may I write a word on the chalkboard?"

"Yes, Gary," I replied. "What word are you going to write?"

"I don't know, but it's got four letters," he said.

"Is it your name?"

"No, it's a word somebody put on my daddy's pickup. The first letter is *F*."

"Uh-oh," I thought. And hesitating between having an obscene word written on the chalkboard or stifling a child's eagerness for learning, I said nothing, realizing that I had no readers in this class. And if it was an obscenity I could quietly caution him that that was not a nice word and he should forget it.

So, as I held my breath, Gary took chalk and carefully wrote his four-letter word on the board:

FORD

* * *

As I walked past the line of children to open the classroom door at dismissal time, I really wasn't prepared to have a five-year-old future Don Juan pinch me on the fanny. (Was he imitating his father's behavior? Or was that sexual harassment in kindergarten?) I ignored it and it was never repeated.

Chapter 47

Real People?

Overheard:
Brad: "Are teachers real people?"
Jose: "Only after school and on Saturdays."

I've told about mistakes that children have made, innocently or otherwise. And I've told about mistakes, or at least unwise things, that parents are guilty of. But does that mean that teachers are perfect? Not by a whole lot! Just like *real people* we sometimes misunderstand, misjudge, overreact, or just plain goof up.

One thing I learned in working with small children is that frequently what at first glance appears to be naughtiness may not be. Sometimes it is; sometimes it ain't! There have been times when I have scolded first, then realized that the child's intentions were innocent. Perhaps he misunderstood directions or perhaps his efforts were misdirected. In any case, I have apologized to the child because I misunderstood his intentions.

* * *

This, from a fellow-teacher's experience, helped confirm this concept in my mind. It was the opening day of school; first grades were large, about thirty per class. It was during the time when we had no kindergartens, so children were less prepared for first grade. To make matters worse, it was *hot*, and our schools were not air-conditioned then.

As part of the getting-acquainted process, Mrs. B. was bringing her children in small groups to sit on the floor around her chair, where they chatted with her and perhaps discussed a large picture of children at play, or pets, or such; something to help her assess their school readiness level. She had met with the first two groups. Then she said to the class, "Now, all those who have not had a turn to do so, please come now and make a nice little circle around my chair."

So the group gathered, and just as they were starting with the discussion, she noticed that Charlie was marking on the floor with his red crayon. This, at the end of a long, hot day, with thirty restless kids. End of patience!

"Charlie, what do you think you are doing? You are supposed to be sitting here in the circle with the other children. You just go wet a paper towel at the sink and scrub those crayon marks off the floor."

So Charlie scrubbed and cried, and, of course, the crayon marks didn't come off. When he told mama about it at home naturally she was upset that her one-and-only got into trouble on his very first day at school. Mom called Mrs. B. and set up an appointment for a conference. Mrs. B. was a young teacher and was nervous about the confrontation she was facing. In her mind she was going over the events leading up to Charlie's misdeed. Suddenly she realized what she had said: "Make a circle around my chair," which was exactly what Charlie had done — with his red crayon.

* * *

I recall an incident when I was a child. The kids in our class had developed a habit which the teacher (rightly) found very annoying. When given a short assignment, such as, "Now read paragraph number 12 silently," the first child finished would invariably raise his hand. The teacher, thinking he had a problem, would say, "Yes, Johnny."

He would reply, "I'm through." This procedure would be repeated by the next one to finish, and the next, and the next.

So one day the teacher gave us quite a sermon about this. We were *not* to raise our hands and say, "I'm through." Then she assigned us a paragraph to read. Upon completing it, little Verna raised her hand and said, "I've finished."

Wow, did I ever catch it! But my intentions were innocent. I thought she meant that "I'm through," was grammatically incorrect, so notice, that's *not* what I said.

* * *

One lesson I learned early in my kindergarten teaching career:

Mary came in from the playground at recess very upset and carrying a button that had come off her overalls strap. I had a needle and thread in my desk drawer, so, no problem, I sewed the button back on, and all was fine.

But the next morning Mary arrived at school wearing a dress with a button missing and holding the button in her little hot hand. "My mama wants you to sew this button on my dress," she said.

I said, "Huh-uh. I teach school. Mamas sew on buttons!" as I fished a safety pin out of my desk drawer and pinned the dress.

After that, yes, I could have easily done little emergency mending jobs with needle and thread, but I didn't. A missing button rated a safety pin, and a hem ripping out got stapled, all with an admonition to be sure to tell Mom that it needed mending.

* * *

Sometimes misunderstandings arise because the child only half listens. I remember Donnie, a handsome child, but with a very negative attitude, something you rarely see in kindergarten. In December, *My Weekly Reader*[1] had a lesson about weather, including snow. I asked the class, "At what time of year might it snow?"

Several children answered, "It snows at Christmas."

I said, "Well, probably not here. In some parts of the country it might, but here where we live it almost never snows at Christmas. If we get snow at all, it usually comes in January."

The next day Donnie announced, "My daddy says you're crazy

if you think it's going to snow at Christmas. It won't snow at Christmas." (At that point I knew where Donnie got his negative attitude.)

I said, "Donnie, perhaps you should learn to listen better. What I said was that we *almost never* get snow at Christmas."

But guess what? That year on Christmas we had a big snow. Even though, strictly speaking, I was wrong, somehow I felt vindicated.

* * *

Sometimes what the teacher says is misinterpreted in another way. When Kathleen was in seventh grade she announced at the dinner table one evening, "Mom, I've got to have a dollar tomorrow for class dues. It was supposed to be in by last Friday. Mr. C. announced today that all class dues have to be paid by tomorrow or they will be *juvenile*."

It took a minute or so to translate that they would be *delinquent*. But she still swears that he said *juvenile*. Perhaps he did. Teachers make mistakes, too.

* * *

Part of my student teaching was labeled "Mexican First Grade," which meant that it was a reading-readiness group with major emphasis on development of an English vocabulary. Today that would be called discrimination and segregation in spite of the fact that it was the most efficient way to help Mexican students gain a working vocabulary in English.

Manuel was a cute little tyke, and one hundred percent mischief. One afternoon Maria kept trying to tell me something, something about Manuel. At that time I had not been around Spanish speaking people enough to develop an ear for the language, especially as spoken by small children. What Maria was saying sounded to me like, "Mon-wale, he essay daba-a-at wert." She repeated it several times, but it still sounded like "Mon-wale, he essay daba-a-at wert." I knew it was something about Manuel, but, of course, he took the Fifth Amendment.

Dismissal time came, and I thought I had dismissed the problem, too. But no, in a few minutes Maria was back accompanied by her older sister, a girl of eight or nine. She was very concerned because, "Mon-wale hee eskal Maria daba-a-at nem." Finally, I deciphered the complaint: Manuel had said a bad word; he had called Maria a bad name.

Now this was definitely something *not* covered in any methods course I had taken; I was strictly left strictly to my own meager resources. And what I did was probably not the best option: I asked , "Well, what was the word?" Thinking maybe it wasn't really a bad word, maybe she just thought it was. Big Sister looked embarrassed and then gave me a word in Spanish. I was still totally unenlightened, so I asked, "What does it mean in English?" She shuffled her feet, hesitated, and then said, "Oh, Mees, I do not kno-o-w how to sa-a-y, but it ees som'teeng like a dog." I got the message.

* * *

Sometimes teachers cause misunderstanding by using idiomatic expressions that a child doesn't understand, or that he takes literally. I remember saying something like, "We will *not* be dismissed until *everyone* gets the papers picked up around his chair, even if we have to stand here 'til the cows come home'." Even the ranch kids didn't quite understand that, unless they had milk cows, too.

* * *

I remember Rosa, a darling little black girl, sweet, capable, always well groomed, and well-liked by all. Smart enough, but she had not learned to use the scissors. I had worked with her, using the training scissors (a double-handled pair that enables both child and teacher to operate them together). My aide had worked with her; volunteer aides had tried to help her. But the truth was, she had made up her mind that she couldn't or wouldn't learn to cut.

This had gone on until December. On this particular day we were doing a cut-and-paste project. My aide and I circulated around the class helping or encouraging each child. Each time I came to Rosa, there she sat making no effort to cut. I would help her enough to get her started, I thought, but the next time around, there she sat; still no progress. The others were finishing the project and cleaning up, and it was nearly bell time. Others were lining up, and still she sat, not even trying.

I said, "Rosa, this has gone on long enough. *You are going to learn to cut.*"

She looked up at me and said, "Miz Chambers, Ah hates you!"

I said, "I'm sorry that you feel that way, Rosa, because I love you. But the fact remains, you *are* going to learn to cut, *even if we have to stay here all night!*"

I turned around and took care of dismissing the class. When I returned to Rosa, she had managed to cut (okay, mangle) whatever it was. At least she had made an effort. We got the pasting done quickly, and she went on her way.

The next morning, guess who was the first child in my classroom? Rosa, who with a big smile, rushed in to give me a big hug. Then she busied herself at the paint easel. About that time Danny, the usual early bird, entered. He greeted me, then spied Rosa. "Hey, Rosa, you're here early this morni. . . ." Then his mouth dropped open and his eyes got big with wonder. And he finished with, ". . . or did you have to stay here all night?" (Rosa learned to use the scissors after that incident.)

* * *

Another case of confusion caused by the use of a colloquial expression: One day a mother, a friend of mine, came to me with a carefully worded question about her son's fourth-grade teacher. I replied something to the effect that I thought Mrs. X. was a good teacher, rather different in personality, but certainly all right. Then she came out with what was really on her mind. It seemed that Johnny had reported, "Mom, I don't understand my teacher. Mrs. X. got mad and said to us, 'Now boys, this business of having to go to the restroom as soon as you come in after lunch is nonsense, and it's got to stop. Don't think you can spend all lunch time playing, and then take class time to go to the rest room. Beginning today, you be sure you use the rest room *before* the bell rings because I'm not going to let you be excused. If you need to go after class starts, that's just too bad. You'll just have to *stick it out* 'till recess.' And Mom, I don't know what she means!"

* * *

Is it possible that a teacher can be just plain wrong about something? Well, how about this? The music instructor was teaching my first graders the Christmas song, "Up on the Housetop," by B. R. Hanly. You remember — it begins "Up on the housetop the reindeer pause." One child asked, "What does 'pause' mean?"

The music teacher replied, "Oh, that's their feet. You know, paws, furry feet like dogs and cats have."

I thought, "Horrors!", but one doesn't contradict another teacher in front of the class. (As a matter of fact, this particular teacher was not someone I would differ with at any time.) However, the next day as I was practicing the class on that song I was able to explain and demonstrate the meaning of "pause" without making any reference to the misinformation given them the day before. And I casually mentioned that deer have hooves like cows.

* * *

I suppose this could be called "Don't Underestimate the Little Rascals!" Mrs. J. had an unusually unruly class, with most of the problems being stirred up by one we'll call Sean. One day Mrs. M., the music teacher, arrived just in time to find that class in a real uproar. The children were told to put their heads down and practice being quiet, and the two teachers waited as the children quieted down and the tension relaxed. Sean, true to form, was only semi-cooperative. Mrs. J. said softly to Mrs. M., "That one is a real S-T-I-N-K-E-R!"

The comment didn't escape sharp-eared little Bryan who sat in the nearest seat. He added, "Yeah, and he's a real P-E-S-T, too!"

And the moral of this story is:
Be careful of the words you spell,
And watch the ear that hears;
The words you spell you may spell well,
But small pitchers have big ears!

* * *

The big moment had arrived... the evening of the big Christmas program. The children were dressed in their holiday best and full of anticipation, and the teachers were thinking, "Thank goodness, the children are really behaving well, taking their parts seriously. And they all know their lines."

Backstage the teachers carefully lined up the children holding the large letters they were to carry which would spell: "CHRISTMAS STAR." The children marched themselves out with amazing decorum and lined themselves up as they were sent. But alas! the teacher who lined up the "S T A R" children sent them out in reverse order, and there they stood in all their glory:

* * *

So what more can I say? If "to err is human" teachers must be as human as the children they teach, as well as the rest of earth's inhabitants. And surely those with even a spark of divinity will forgive us our trespasses.

* * *

If, in spite of my having changed all names, and sometimes the gender of all persons described here, you think you recognize yourself, you can:
a. Vehemently deny it.
b. Look innocent and ask, "Johnny *who?*"
c. Look smug and say, "I know who that was, but I'm not telling."

d. Admit it and brag.
e. Admit it and blush.
f. Just keep quiet because, after all, the statute of limitations has run out.

Works Cited

1. *My Weekly Reader* (children's newspaper). Education Center, Columbus, OH 43216.
2. *Old Testament*, Ecclesiastes.
3. White, Burton, *Educating the Infant and Toddler*, Free Press. 1987.
4. Gesell, Arnold, M.D., *The First Five Years*. Also *The Child from Five to Ten*, w/Frances Ilg, M.D., and Louise Bates Ames, Ph.D. Harper Row, 1977.
5. *Highlights Magazine*. Highlights for Children, Columbus, OH.
6. *Sesame Street Magazine*, Children's Television Workshop, Boulder, CO 80322.
7. Levinson, Harold, M.D., *A Solution to the Riddle - Dyslexia*, Springer-Verlag, 1980, is suggested reading.
8. *The First Grade Book*, (music book), "I'm a Little Teapot", by Clarence Kelley and George H. Sanders. Ginn, 1949.
9. Goodenough, Florence L., *Measurement of Intelligence by Drawings*. Ayer, 1975.
10. *New Testament*, Gospel of John.
11. Arlie Duff, "Y'All Come". Starrite Publishing Co., 1953.
12. *U.S. News & World Report*, July 1, 1996, "Letters" P.7.
13. Dobson, James, Ph.D., *Dare to Discipline*, 1970. Also, *The New Dare to Discipline*, 1992. Tyndale House Publishers, Wheaton, IL.
14. *Fun with Dick and Jane*, also *We Look and See*, etc. Scott Foresman & Co., Chicago, IL.

Suggested Reading

Driekers, Rudolph, *Children, the Challenge*. Hawthorne Books, New York.

Driekers, Rudolph. *Psychology in the Classroom*. Harper & Row, New York.

Leman, Kevin, *The Birth Order Book*. Fleming H. Revell, Old Tappan, New Jersey, 1985.

Leman, Kevin, *Making Children Mind without Losing Yours*. Fleming H. Revell, Old Tappan, New Jersey.

Verna Chambers, An Autobiography

I was born in Pryor, Oklahoma, on November 16, 1921. Now, while it is true that I was the sixth child born to William Jesse and Willeah (Ghormley) Lafferty, it is not true that they just gave me the Roman Numeral VI, and let me choose a name to fit as initials. Had I been given the chance, Verna Ivadell would not have been my choice. Nevertheless, both the name and I have survived.

My father, a construction engineer at heart, was trying his hand at farming when I was quite small. However, he gave this up and returned to the building industry before I reached school age. For a few years my mother maintained our home in Tahlequah, Oklahoma, with my father being wherever his work took him. After Child I and Child II had finished college, and with Child III in college, our parents decided it would be better for the family to move about with my father. Hence, a good part of my growing-up years were spent *a la* gypsy.

My high school work was spread out over three states and five years. I finally managed to graduate from Poly High in Fort Worth, Texas, in 1938, at the age of sixteen. I attended Texas Women's University at Denton, and Arizona State University at Tempe, Arizona. In 1942 I received my B.A. from ASU with a home economics major and a science minor. And there I stood, diploma in hand, and was expected to become self-supporting. With three other teachers in the family, it was natural that I turned in that direction. I began my career in Texas, teaching home economics, chemistry and science in high school, barely older than some of my students. I bought a pair of horn-rimmed glasses and some grannie shoes, and hid my birth certificate until I turned twenty-one.

A romance that began my senior year in college culminated in marriage to Louis Clell Chambers in 1944. When the war was over in 1945, we came to Willcox, Arizona, which was home to Clell. My last year of high school teaching was in Willcox. We then spent four years at Fort Grant, Arizona, at that time the

Arizona State Industrial School for Boys. My husband operated the power plant, and I taught the boys (inmates) for two years during that time. That should have earned me a degree in abnormal psychology.

Our daughter Kathleen was born in 1949, and I finally grew up. We returned to Willcox in 1950, and I entered a new teaching area — kindergarten. With a little one of my own, young children had become fascinating. Except for a two-year leave when our son, Benjamin, was born in 1953, I taught small children until my retirement in 1983. That was six years in first grade, the remainder in kindergarten.

Meanwhile, Clell was operating the ranch, his birthplace, along with his parents. Upon their death in 1961, we moved back into his childhood home. A ranch is a wonderful place to raise children, and I have always enjoyed living on the ranch. But I will be the first to admit that, while I am a rancher's wife, I've never really been a ranch wife. There *is* a difference.

While in college I envisioned that I would be a high school teacher, and I am glad that I had that experience. Although I just stumbled into kindergarten teaching, I found it most rewarding. I liked first grade, but for me it was quite stressful. (What if a child left my first grade still unable to read?) However, the six years that I taught first grade enabled me to be a better kindergarten teacher because I was more keenly aware of the children's needs.

Our daughter became a teacher also — choral music at junior high level. Son Benjamin is a mechanical engineer with Motorola.

Other interests in our lives included church activities, state and local historical societies, and Alpha Delta Kappa. Clell was also involved in Civil Air Patrol and Arizona Cattle Growers' Association. His hobby was electronics, and mine have been oil painting and quilting. And we both loved square dancing. Looking back over the years, I must say there is little I would change, except to have had Clell with me a little longer. He passed away during the preparation of this book. We had a good life together.

POSTSCRIPT-----the REST of the Story:

   I never expected to remarry, but after two weeks alone I happened to meet up with Frank Jordan, a fellow-educator whom I had known casually since the days when I was teaching high school. After I begun teaching kindergarten I was his daughter's first teacher. And later still he was my daughter's high school principal.

   After what is best described as "a 51-year friendship and a 51-day courtship" we married. We find that with the many similarities in background and experiences in education Frank and I have much to share and enjoy in our "sunset years" together.